..NOSIS:

.HE GREEN PATH

,

.

Verdant Gnosis:
Cultivating the Green Path

Edited by Catamara Rosarium and
Jenn Zahrt, PhD

Rubedo Press
2015

Viridis Genii Editions
© Rubedo Press 2015.

Rubedo Press
Seattle, WA
www.rubedo.press

Book and Cover Design by Joseph Uccello.

ISBN 978-1-943710-05-8
First published by Rubedo Press in 2015.
Printed in the United States of America.

TABLE OF CONTENTS

LIST OF FIGURES

Introduction

Simultaneously hidden and revealed, the *Viridis Genii* is the green spirit, intelligence, and ineffable life force—the green gnosis one receives from their deep connection and communion with the *genius loci*. It is the animating force of the wild wood and the depths of the sea. It shrouds us, engulfs us with its veiled green mist, awakening the heartbeat that delivers fecundity to the earth, the very essence of life.

The *Viridis Genii* Symposium explores of the greater mysteries of the Herbal Arte and how it manifests within all traditions, cultures, and practices—the Craft of the Wise. We seek to surpass the mundane and plumb the depths of the green mysteries, fostering an environment where they thrive, nourish, and become one.

Deep within these mysteries, among the magic, among the myths, we find doorways, pathways, and keys, which allow us to enter heavenly worlds and guide us through chthonic realms. In the *Viridis Genii* we find a great teacher, a master in these hidden arts, a liberator. It reveals the secret workings of the world, showing us how to create change behind the veil with the aid of those many green beings, which form the body of the green spirit.

By attending to cycles of the plant world we gain wisdom through vine, flower, root; through seed, thorn, leaf; through bark, branch, and rod. Through this gnosis we are shown how to make charms, healing formulas, and tinctures. We are taught secret teachings and ancient lore of the *genii*. Each is immensely laden with powers and virtues to assist us in blessing and in bane. Powders, potions, incense, and oils; talismans, fetishes, poppets, and charms—we make them all with the body of the *Viridis Genii*.

Through these forces we are given tools to clothe, feed, shelter, and heal. It arouses us to lustful frenzy, aiding us in making love, birthing children, and providing protection. The *Viridis Genii* gives us everything, including our body, as we consume its flesh to make our own.

Through the Viridis Genii Symposium, we wish to cultivate a space where the following subjects cross-pollinate: herbal alchemy; wortcunning; ethnobotany and the magical use of plants; wildcrafting with spirit; herbal astrology; medicine with a focus on spiritual herbal practice; shamanry; witchcraft; indigenous traditional plant wisdom; entheogenic studies and ritual practice; the role of plants in ceremonial magical traditions; herbal charms and talismans; artists whose body of work focuses on plants; craft brewers and distillers. Any topic related to working with plants from the perspective of magic, mysticism, and medicine is welcome, although we prefer to emphasize folk magic, healing, and traditions.

This book is the first volume of the new *Viridis Genii* Editions series. Each year we intend to publish a book containing outstanding articles from presentations delivered at the *Viridis Genii* Symposium. This volume contains articles from nine of the seventeen presenters at the inaugural symposium held at Damascus, Oregon from July 31 to August 2, 2015.

We have selected works based on the spirit they invoke, the distinct thread that weaves the green gnosis into the great tapestry of the green art. The approaches presented here range from the scholarly (Hathaway Diaz) to the poetic (Wazka). Yet each also partakes in the perilous act of attempting to render in language something that necessarily escapes it. We hope that as the reader meanders through the pathways presented, the slippage in the spaces between the words and concepts allows another dimension to emerge. A distinct logic adheres in the plant realm; the repetitions appearing across the essays here evince a knowing that resists articulation in human language. It is a way of knowing that must be experienced directly, and the authors brave enough to share their wisdom reveal their dance around this elusive reality.

One must read carefully across these essays to fully perceive the force of what has been shared. The variety of tone and style demonstrate the myriad entryways to the green path. This book, a celebration of just a few of them, will leave the reader with specific recipes for intentional work with plants, testimony from living practitioners of traditions near and far, and a palpable sense of our inescapable embeddedness in the *Viridis Genii*. It is our hope that this volume serves as a keepsake for the symposium participant and as continued inspiration for the aspirant.

Go well,
Catamara Rosarium, &
Jenn Zahrt, PhD
Olympia, Washington
June 20, 2015

Taxus Baccata

Yew

Green Gold:

Alchemy in the Plant Realm

Robert Allen Bartlett

To broach the subject of alchemy in a short space is a difficult task. There are so many ideas, opinions, and conjectures
as to just what alchemy is all about; is it proto-chemistry or
pseudo-science, a spiritual path or a psychological metaphor,
fact or fiction? This debate is nothing new, it has been going on
for centuries and yet alchemy continues to fascinate all who
venture into its dark waters. Part of the problem lies in the
literature itself, which is filled with symbol, myth, metaphor,
and analogy. If you lack a proper key, it is easy to become lost
in a labyrinth of uncertainty and despair. Another part of the
problem with understanding the intentions of alchemy is that
it crosses all the artificial lines that have become enmeshed
in modern society. The lines between science, magic, and re-
ligion, or mind and matter take on a whole new dimension
within the Hermetic Corpus.

Alchemy has been called the perennial philosophy, Sacred
Science, and Divine Art; going in and out of vogue for centuries, and so it is today that the study of alchemy is gain-
ing worldwide interest in both popular and academic circles.
There exists a massive body of alchemical information available to all unlike at no other time in history. Indeed histories

are being rewritten without the biases of past interpretations, and much of what we were taught about the pseudo-scientific or fraudulent nature of alchemy are now seen as false or at least incomplete descriptions.

In the following pages we will examine some of the basics of alchemical theory and practice especially as applied to the vegetable kingdom, and discuss the why and how of plant alchemy from the perspective of the practicing laboratory alchemist. The old masters admonish us to "know the theory first before attempting the praxis", otherwise we are just bumping around in a laboratory without any guidance.

Alchemy has been called the search for perfection and the search for the quintessence. Twentieth century alchemist Frater Albertus defined alchemy as "consciously assisted evolution". Far from being a mad quest to turn base metals into gold, alchemy is a philosophy, an exploration of the true nature of reality, our place in that picture and the practical applications of that knowledge. The origins of alchemy are still the center of hot debate, with China, India, and Egypt as major contenders. East and West certainly influenced the development of core alchemical theories. For the West, alchemy is considered to be the product of ancient Egyptian technical skills and mysticism with Greek philosophy, which took place around 200 BCE in Alexandria.

The ancient Greek philosophers, most of whom studied for many years in the Egyptian mystery schools, sought to clarify and summarize the nature of reality, how things come into existence and ultimately decay. Alchemists from all ages say we must follow in the footsteps of nature for "Our Art" to be successful and the concepts of nature from such great luminaries as Pythagoras, Socrates, Plato, and Aristotle held full sway over alchemical thought well into the eighteenth century.

Some of the most important ideas from Greek philosophy

which helped shape the theory and practice of alchemy include foremost the concept that all we perceive in our everyday world is derived from one source. "One is All" became a fundamental mantra and stable foundation for the development of philosophies concerned with the operations of Nature. The idea that all things are moving toward a state of greater perfection is another central concept throughout the alchemical corpus, today we might think of this as the force of natural evolution. Closely related to this are the recurring themes of the celestial ascent of the soul and the separation of souls from bodies. The concept of four elemental states and a trinity of powers within the One resulted in a conception of the elemental constitution of materials as embodiments of those spiritual principles and set the stage for development of ideas concerning transmutation from one material into another with its ultimate perfection in mind.

The ancient philosophers postulated an infinite ocean of living mind containing the forms of all creation in potential. All of the elemental qualities within the One in total balance, no one taking precedence over another, static, nothing can happen, and in a sense it does not really exist. The ancients called this the One, the All, Chaos, Divine Intellect, Prima Materia, Celestial Fire and many other similar titles. We can symbolize the concept but cannot comprehend this state of unity. "The Tao which can be named is not the Tao".

The One, reflecting on itself, begins the first motion towards polarity and thereby to expressing itself. Now we get contrast. One pole compared to the other or acting on the other is the condition required for us to understand. Modern science recognizes the unity of energy and matter which the ancients described as Spirit and Matter or Aristotle's Form and Matter. Matter did not really exist until it was impressed with a Form or more exactly a Substantial Form (from which

13

we derive our term, substance). This Form was the real Soul of the thing not just how it looked but the formative energy behind its entire life cycle and purpose for being. But Form and Matter are codependent; one does not exist without the other. The One becomes two and the three aspects together become the fundamental package of essentials for a thing to exist. At its highest level of expression, this is the trinity inherent within the One; expressing the divine attributes of omniscience, omnipotence, and omnipresence. The One as ultimate Spirit or intellect has within itself an energetic mode and material mode, the three being anciently designated as Spirit, Soul, and Body or as the alchemists termed them Mercury, Sulfur, and Salt. To the alchemist, everything that exists possesses a body, soul, and spirit; even those things we do not usually associate with such concepts as a plant or lump of rock. In modern terms, we might describe these three essentials as matter, energy, and intelligence.

The familiar hermetic axiom "As above, so below" from the *Emerald Tablet of Hermes Trismegistus* guides us to an understanding that these spiritual principles have their reflection here in the material world with affinities to certain types and states of matter. Nature is a continuum from the most dense to the most subtle essences and the ancient hermetic philosophers perceived the cyclic process of Nature whereby One becomes the many and the many return to the One.

The physical world is just one layer (the most dense or fixed part) of a much larger macrocosm which includes layers of spiritual intelligence or archetypal forms, rational and instinctive levels of mind, as well as an electromagnetic signature. Greek philosophy mentions these various levels as the Intellectual world, the Celestial world, and the Elemental world; while the cabbalistic student refers to four interconnected worlds of increasing subtlety. In the East, Indian alchemists speak of the several sheaths or subtle bodies which enclose a spark of the divine present in all things; each sheath rooted in a different level of reality.

One of the most important goals of the alchemical work is the perfection of an incorruptible body, represented by gold in the metallic realm. Variously termed the "Spiritual Body", the "Diamond Body", "Glorified Corpus", and "the Immortal Body", it is the true Form of the individual. From the most ancient times, preservation or mummification of the physical body in order to provide a deceased entity an access to the physical world has been practiced worldwide. Early alchemical investigators sought out methods of creating an incorruptible body of spiritualized matter that could be occupied while still here, alive and coextending a physical body. This goal was one of the primary occupations of earliest Chinese and Indian alchemists, who directly influenced each other and the West in the pursuit of "The Elixir of Life"; a substance that could cure disease, extend the lifespan, and bring about illumination in a spiritualized body. Research along this line developed a large class of materials purported to have restorative and rejuvenative properties. These materials were called *rasayanas* by Indian alchemists and included plant, animal, and mineral derivatives, while Chinese alchemists produced an array of colorfully named elixirs such as "Grand Unity Jade Powder Elixir", mostly of mineral origin. While many of these materials were recognized as not being the Grand Elixir, their value was seen in extending the artist's lifespan in order to buy more time to complete the Great Alchemical Work. Examples of Indian *rasayanas* from the plant realm include the more familiar ginseng, gotu kola, and fo ti along with more exotic plants as ashwagandha, pippali, haritaki, brahmi, guggulu resin, amalaki, bhringaraj and triphala. In the West, the writings of Paracelsus contain several tracts which address life extension where the properties of the plants melissa and celandine are held in high esteem as containing an abundance of a rejuvenative quintessence. One favorite combination mentioned was that of aloe, saffron, and myrrh confected into an "Elixir Proprietatis" said to be nearly as powerful as the Grand Elixir itself. All of these materials are readily available to the practicing alchemist and can be processed into valuable medicines with healing and rejuvenative powers whose action extends beyond just the physical body, but can affect soul and spirit levels as well.

This brings us to the laboratory works of the alchemist. Some will contend that there is no real laboratory tradition in alchemy, that it is all about psychology and metaphor. However it then becomes difficult to explain the existence of alchemical laboratories distributed throughout the world. That the alchemists were working with material substances in a unique manner has been indicated by numerous studies and authors. Was it just protochemistry? In some cases, yes, but there has always been a line of alchemists guided by a more esoteric philosophy, the philosophy of Nature from the alchemical viewpoint.

The alchemical laboratory is a place where theory is put to the test. Very often insights into the workings of nature are very deeply impressed in the mind of the worker because seeing the changes that occur in the laboratory to the work at hand provides powerful subconscious messages which are processed and lead to further insights and illumination of the work. The key process or method used in the laboratory is based on nature's own process in the macrocosmic world. This process was termed Spagyria by Paracelsus, derived from Greek words meaning to separate and reunite, which is a rewording of the older alchemical adage *solve et coagula*.

In his writings, Paracelsus outlines the nature of the physical representatives of spiritual principles or the physical cloaks of non-physical realities to be met with in the laboratory, he says:

> Everything which is generated of its elements is divided into three, namely into Salt, Sulfur, and Mercury. Learn the form which is peculiar to these three. One is liquor and this is the form of Mercury; one is oiliness and this is the form of Sulfur; one is alkali and this is the form of Salt.

The following table will help to summarize the nature of the three essentials from their spiritual origin from the One to their physical counterparts.

OMNIPRESENCE	OMNIPOTENCE	OMNISCIENCE
MATTER	ENERGY	INTELLIGENCE
BODY	SOUL	SPIRIT
SALT	SULFUR	MERCURY
ALKALI SALT	OIL	VOLATILE LIQUOR

Although we are mainly concerned here with vegetable works in alchemy, these principles apply to all three realms—animal, vegetable, and mineral. The Spagyric process is subdivided into three main steps. The first step is separation of a material's essential components in the form of a crude spirit, soul, and body. These components are then purified using a variety of methods available to the laboratory worker. Finally the purified body soul and spirit are reunited into a new homogeneous matter free from corruptibility as a perfected form of the original substance. In short, the steps are labeled as separation, purification, and cohobation. An example will illustrate.

To begin we select the plant which is traditionally held to be naturally high in life-giving quintessence such as melissa or celandine, or alternatively the qualities of a *rasayana* in eastern medicine. Preferably, and for a true alchemical result, the plant chosen should be still living, harvested quickly, and immediately placed into processing. Most alchemical works, and this is true of the herbal works especially, begin with the process of putrefaction. It is only in death that things will give up their spiritual principles. This is known as philosophical death in the laboratory. In nature things will die and decay and their constituents will be dispersed back into nature. In the alchemist's laboratory the spiritual components are trapped in a vessel they cannot escape from, sometimes referred to as a glass coffin. So the plant is allowed to die and ferment and in doing so it gives up the ghost, the volatile spiritual constituents. This process is one of reverting the vegetable material into its own vegetable chaos or Prima Materia. It is said that things will resolve themselves into that of which they were made; so this vegetable chaos represents the elements that were brought together under the action of the Substantial Form/Sulfur, which resulted in the plant itself.

We take now this vegetable chaos and place it into a retort and gradually apply heat. The first thing that rises is a volatile spirit; this is labeled as the alchemical Mercury and set aside. Now the heat is increased gradually, and water will start to come over—this is called the flood. Soon the water will become colored and sour, smoke will arise followed by drops of thick black oil. This combustible oil represents the alchemical Sulfur in a crude state. What remains in our retort is a lump of black charcoal in which are hidden the pure mineral salts or the body of the plant. We have now separated the three essential portions of the plant, its body, soul, and spirit. The next step of the Spagyric process is that of purification. The volatile Mercury and thick black oil are redistilled several times to purify and spiritualize them. The charcoal which remained at the bottom of the retort is placed into a hot furnace and calcined into a white ash which represents the true body of the plant. Once these three essential ingredients have been purified, all of their external hindrances, accidents, and dysfunctionality have been removed.

Now, in a sort of resurrection, the mineral salts, the body of the plant, are reunited with its purified Sulfur and Mercury to create what alchemist Isaac Holland called a "Glorified Corpus", able to express the plant's true character without any hindrances or distortion. This process described above goes under the general term of Spagyric Anatomy which is discussed in great detail in the work, *Golden Chain of Homer*. In contemporary alchemical works there are additional ways of going about this process of creating alchemical elixirs. One common method is to first steam distill out the volatile essential oil which represents the spiritual Sulfur of the plant; this is very delicate, and it is removed first so that during the next step (which is the fermentation of the residue), this delicate oil is not destroyed. Once we have obtained the oil, the residue is placed into fermentation where it gives up its spirit into the watery medium; this spirit or Mercury is now distilled and captured. All that remains is dried and calcined into a white ash and so once again we have our body, soul, and spirit separated and purified, ready to recombine into a Glorified Corpus. Now, all of this laboratory work may seem daunting to one just beginning their alchemical journey; but take heart, for there are still more simple methods available to all, which use common materials and appliances. These simple methods will serve to get you manually involved in laboratory works with little expense and provide experiences which may lead to valuable insights to the works of Nature. At least you will be able to tell if laboratory alchemy piques your interest enough to actively pursue more advanced works, and it will provide you with valuable medicinal agents and initiatory tools along the way.

The following description for producing a Spagyric extract of a plant relies on the main constituent of the volatile spirit of the vegetable realm: alcohol. When we go to the liquor store we purchase "spirits", vegetable spirits. We still use this term from the alchemical past. This being the case, we can simply buy a strong alcohol to act as the plant spirit or vegetable Mercury, one of our three essentials. The Mercury of a kingdom has a powerful affinity for the Sulfur of that kingdom, so we will use the alcohol to extract the Sulfur of the chosen plant thus effecting a separation of the plant's essentials.

Select a plant or even a combination of plants you wish to work on; they can be fresh or dried in this experiment. Chop, crush, or grind the herbs then place an ounce or two into a large glass jar with a tight-fitting lid. Pour the alcohol you have purchased (100 proof vodka or Everclear are good choices) over the herbs until it swims about half an inch above the level of the herbs. Seal the jar and shake it well; then place into a warm spot to digest (100–105 degrees F is ideal). Set the jar to digest like this for one or two weeks with occasional shaking. After the two weeks, filter the liquid out into another container using a coffee filter and funnel. Set this liquid aside; it contains the Mercury and Sulfur of the plant in a more concentrated and purified form. The extracted plant residue is placed into a fireproof dish and incinerated outside into as white an ash as possible. After the initial burn, the ash may be placed under an oven broiler to bring it to a lighter shade. The ash is ground into powder and then added directly to the liquid extract, which was collected earlier. Seal the vessel which now contains the Mercury, Sulfur, and Salt of the original plant(s) and again set it to digest another week or longer. At the end of the time period, the material is once again filtered and now ready for use. If you would like to carry this simple experiment further and produce an even more powerful transformative agent, you can place the ash of the plant into a vial then imbibe the ash with drops of the liquid extract just until it is saturated; seal and digest. As the liquid is absorbed and the matter appears dry, add more of the liquid extract and continue the digestion. After about a month, remove the matter and calcine it again in a fireproof dish. Collect and grind the resulting white solid, then return it to the glass vial. Now the process of imbibing and digestion is repeated for a new cycle. After many cycles the matter will become like a stone, the Vegetable Stone, with highly augmented powers of the original herbs. The final result then will be a solid of which only a small fragment is necessary for consumption.

To what end are we making these alchemical elixirs and what are their effects? We mentioned the term *rasayana* as being related to the effects of regeneration, rejuvenation, and extension of life. They act in extending the life so that we have additional time available to accomplish the Great Work. In his commentary to the *Triumphal Chariot of Antimony* by Basil Valentine, Dr. Theodor Kerckring comments on the activity of these medications and though he's speaking directly of antimony preparations what he says also applies to these vegetable-based materials; he says:

> these medicaments do not work sensibly as emetics, cathartics and sudorifics are wont to do but, insensibly by uniting their own more purified universal spirit with our own spirit, amending Nature and restoring Health.

Spagyric medicines are held to be "living medicines" and evolved representatives of the species they are derived from. As such they can express the material's true healing character without distortion caused by impurities or other dysfunctions picked up during the individual's lifetime. In addition to this, they operate as a higher intelligence and thus have a greater command over lower functions.

The healing benefits are one aspect of these alchemical preparations, but there is another side to them: that of their initiatory quality, that is, of their ability to open up alternate states of awareness to bring insight into the workings of Nature and our place in it. Spagyric extracts have been used extensively as sacraments in magical works in order to gain access to various levels of Nature from the physical to the spiritual heights. They are not toys in this context and should be used with due preparation. The unprepared have complained of various psychic disturbances from old memories or life lessons we need to address, and this can be unsettling; however it is part of our own purification and evolution which these extracts accelerate.

We have barely scratched at the surface of the venerable art of alchemy here. If the Sacred Science calls to you, it is still easy to get lost in the mass of information available on the internet. It would help to find a qualified guide to get you started in the right direction, and there are a number of schools—mostly based on the teachings of Frater Albertus of Paracelsus College fame, or of the French group, The Philosophers of Nature—that can fill that need.

As the "Mother of all art and science" the study of alchemy leads to a lifetime of discovery and revelation about Nature's operations and how to manipulate matter and situations toward perfection based on that higher knowledge.

The Genius in the Bottle:

Bioregional Animism and the Viridis Genii

Marcus McCoy

Congress with spirits has been sought by some humans since the beginning of human history. Shamans, *goēs*, witches, sorcerers, mediums, and many other titles for those who practice what has come to be called magic, have sought the aid of intelligent forces to assist in their pursuits. This practice continues today across cultural divides, traditions, and currents, and though the act may take on myriad forms, it still moves on, unabated, evolving along with us, and yet staying close to its unimaginable origins.

For the practitioner of herbal magic, the act of having congress with the intelligence of plants is of equal importance. Intermediaries are frequently sought out to aid in the communication between plant spirits and humans. Plant teachers, and communicator species such as Ayahuasca, have in the last several decades become a holy grail for seekers who wish to have congress with spirits, and communicate with a plant. The number of tours to South American jungles and articles in major magazines on the subject shows now more than ever the intriguing notion and possible importance of plant/human communication.

The plant magician, healer, and sorcerer all seek congress

with a living embodied spirit, much like themselves, but a green feral kind, with an intelligence that remains a mystery to us. A mystery, if perpetuated, brings the gifts of healing, divination, wisdom and growth, as well as darker needs and power.

Since 2006 I have written on the subject of bioregional animism, a conceptual gift from the land to me that I shared with others, attempting to help them establish communion with their larger biotic self, the life-place, or bioregion in which they live their daily existence. A foundational concept within bioregional animism is in that of the *genius loci*, the spirit of place, an intelligence composed of the entire biotic community within a specific bioregion. As the human body is composed of flora and fauna and innumerable cells, each informed by the others and working in synergy, one might also find that entire ecosystems are living sentient bodies composed of larger intelligent bodies of various kinds.

The *genius loci* is the spirit of the bioregion or life place itself. Its animated intelligence is the collected soul and mind of all that composes it within the bioregion and that which at the same time animates and gives mind and soul to those living within the bioregion. Every human, plant, microbe, snail, and four legged animal is one with the *genius loci* that comprise the bioregion itself. All within the *genius loci* are at the same time autonomous aspects of that whole. Within the practice of bioregional animism, *one works to find inner oneness with the larger self, the land that animates us*, and to work in synergy with it/as it.

What then is the *viridis genii*? The translation of *viridis genii* is the green spirit which is there for the collective autonomous force that animates the green world within the bioregion, the soul of the forest, swamp, desert, and prairie plants, and all of the green growing things composing the *genius loci*. Every tree, fern, blade of grass, whether native or introduced, that grows within the natural boundaries of a bioregion, collectively makes up the intelligence of the *viridis genii*. The *viridis genii* is wise beyond words. There is not a single herbalist, alchemist, or even scientist that has not gloried in wonder at its vast intelligence and wisdom. Though it be called and known in other ways, morphogenetic fields, the glory of god, evolution, or attributed to some pagan deity from some other far off land, its glory is still known. What is important however to the wortcunner, the magical herbalist, is again the congress with spirits, and in this case specifically plant spirits.

From a bioregional animist standpoint, being a relational ontology, we relate to this larger composite intelligence that is the *viridis genii* as a person, not a human person, but an other than human person. We are not anthropomorphizing the *viridis genii*, but instead recognizing its innate personhood. Animism recognizes that humans are not the only persons in the world after all.

The *viridis genii* is a different person to all of us, just as I am a different person to everyone because of the nature of relationship itself. Magical herbalists come from a great many other worldviews and perceptions of the spiritual and physical world, and thus have different ways of relating to the *viridis genii*. Therefore the *viridis genii* will have different ways of relating to these individual practitioners of the green arts. Some may relate to the *viridis genii* as the one, and inseparable from the *genius sanguinarius*, the blood spirit—flora and fauna interwoven—but that is beyond my scope here. Regardless of how our relationship with the *viridis genii* takes shape, if we relate to it as a person we can meet with the *genii* and commune with them so that the *genii* will in return commune back.

Again we return to the practitioner of magic's desire to seek congress with spirits, as practitioners of the green arts we understand the importance of communion. How is the *viridis genii* met? How does one seek congress with them? Many paths exist, many ways within the green arts, and many traditions and practices, but here I share from the perspective and experience of the bioregional animist. By relating to the *viridis genii* as an other than human person, we accept that persons communicate and are intelligent. Through relating to the *viridis genii* as a person we take our first steps towards contact. The next step is through relating to the other than human person as we would with other persons: from a place of respect. The *viridis genii* is also much larger than we are, and it gives us that which we need to live. Our homes are often made of it, our clothing, our food, the paper on which we write (and, verily, this book in your hands), the medicines we take to live, our very bodies are here and composed of this amazing person. We owe our life to it. It is a teacher, a healer, and has lived on this planet far longer than humans, far longer than even mammals. It is our elder, and so we also relate to this person with humility.

This humility is very important in establishing congress, communicating, and communing with the *viridis genii*, and eventually working with this spirit. Out of respect we do not force this *genii* into our bottle. Instead, with humility, we invite it.

THE GENIUS IN THE BOTTLE

The bottle is not a trap; it is the vessel in which it can travel, it is a spirit house for the *genii*—the bottle is a home for it. We begin by blessing and washing our bottle approximately a quart in size. This bottle is also, in a sense, symbolic of ourselves, for we too as practitioners of the green arts wish to be a vessel for the spirit of the green. So we go to places of pure water, the water that nurtures the green spirit and the plants that compose it. These can be the sources of rivers, streams, deep artesian wells, lakes that are used for a water source because of their purity. Rainwater can be collected in purified and sanctified vessels, or snow can be melted from the tops of mountains.

Many water sources from around the life place should be visited with the same intention of pilgrimage and with respect and humility, for these water sources are also persons, persons we all require for our very lives. Humble offerings of gratitude and reciprocity are given to these water sources, and a small amount of water may be collected from each and then combined within the vessel. No more than a third of the bottle should be filled with this holy water to which we owe so much.

Offerings can be traditional from your path, and or can be the simple offering of one's hair. Too grandiose an offering lacks humility in the relationship of giving. The offering of a goat, for example, will probably not be required. One's spittle, urine, or other bodily fluids can also be offered as an act of returning one's water back to the source, a completion of the circle of sacred reciprocity. These offerings indeed must be humble and slight.

Next visit the study of the alchemists, the distillers, and those who emulate natural process as the praxis of their tradition. Here we require access to the *aqua vitae*—the water of life, alcohol, EtOH, also known to many as spirits. Alcohol is essential to many who work within the green arts. It is well known, though some do not work with it and choose other methods. Ethanol is revered not only for its preservative properties but for its ability to work as a solvent, however vegetable oils may also be used in the preparing of this *genii* in a bottle. The reason why vegetable oil is not used in this formula is because water and oil do not mix. The vessels for the *genii* are itself a life place and must include the water that animates us all. Spirits are added not only as a preservative, but also because of the power and magical cycle of life and death inimical to the creation of alcohol itself.

One should therefore ideally collect a plant that is high in sugar that grows within the life place, and request that the *genius viridium* concentrate itself with this plant you are harvesting. This evocation of the green spirit is of utmost importance and should incorporate as much of the knowledge and wisdom of your particular path as a practitioner of the green arts. Again give humble and respectful offerings to these plants. Your goal is to call and invite the green spirit into one's harvest prior to harvesting it. Make sure the tools for cutting or digging also be cleansed and sanctified in your way.

The plants can be edible roots, fresh leaves, vegetables from one's garden, grapes, berries, corn, and wheat; other plants high in sugar will do. Honey can also be used if gathered from one's own hives, as an additive to the fermentation. If honey is used, the bees must be asked permission and also given offerings prior to the extraction of their honey, for they are the pollinators and a great part of the green mysteries. Wild yeasts can be cultivated and or attracted for the fermentation of the plants and added to water, preferably waters gathered from sacred pure sources, again with accompanying offerings.

Once you have collected your plants, then purify and sanctify a small gallon to five-gallon demijohn as your primary fermenter. One would do well to learn the fermenter's arts prior to attempting a wild wine, beer, or mead. With practice, one will learn the art and enjoy it immensely. The importance of this act lies in the plant's death and release from its physical body into the universal solvent that is water—that which once gave the *genii* living form now contains its spirit.

Next we have the illicit act of distillation, where we separate the spirit of the host from the universal solvent that is water. The alcohol created by the fermentation of the vital sugars within the plant now carry the evoked green spirit of the life place. One purifies and sanctifies one's alembic and asks for the water to now release the spirit of the green one directly into one's vessel. Heads and hearts are acceptable for the spirit vessel, for this will not be consumed. If the fermentation took its course well, and if there were sufficient sugars in the plant chosen for fermenting, there should now be enough spirits to fill three fourths of your bottle. The head and hearts are received only. Once the heart is finished distilling, the heat is turned off and what is left within the alembic is given back to the land as an offering after it has cooled.

This is not intended as an instructional guide in the art of distilling or fermenting, as distillation can be relatively dangerous if not done with adequate knowledge and equipment. Know that in many parts of the world, especially the United States where this article is written, that the art of distillation is illegal and controlled, and must be done at the risk of one's own freedom. It is recommended that prior to doing this work, that one has learned enough and gained enough confidence in the art to see it through.

Once our vessel is full of heads and hearts of the green spirit and recombined with sacred waters, we give the green spirit a body. While carrying the vessel into the life place, request the *genius viridium* to guide you to plants that you may ally yourself with to make the foundation of its body within the spirit vessel. Listen to nature, listen to the land, pay attention to how you feel and what you think. This is your guidance. Especially listen to your passive thoughts. This is the birth of the *genius viridum* fetish bottle that will be your guide and tutelary spirit within the green world that is your bioregion.

When you feel led to a plant, ask its permission to harvest. Again, if harvesting with tools be sure they have been purified and sanctified in your way. Invite the plant to live within your spirit vessel and be the body of the spirit within. Give a humble offering in your way to the plant, and harvest only a small amount of the plant to place within the bottle. This bottle will get filled within your lifetime with all of the plants growing within your bioregion that you are drawn to work with, or that introduce themselves to you, so be mindful of how much of the plant is added. Feel free to dedicate a full lunation to this path, or even a full year harvesting plants that can only be harvested seasonally or within particular eco-niches within your bioregion.

Additional methodologies can be venerated during this process of creating the body of the *genius viridium*. Plants can be harvested during specific corresponding planetary elections, and all added during specific beneficial and corresponding astrological times, remembering that wise old adage, "as above so below". Another possible methodology would be to add for the base body of the fetish seven plants, each with correspondences to the seven planets, harvested on the days and hours corresponding with the plants' ruling planets. Plants can also be harvested and added during a year's time on specific venerations of the equinoxes and solstices.

The wisdom of the possible method of adding seven plants to represent all corresponding planets is not to be ignored, for one would have a complete body representing every corresponding field in which the plant world may aid us in our lives. For the cunning distiller, or master of the alchemical process of making herbal spagyrics, a few drops of spagyric of each plant can be added alternately. As always with magic, the possibilities are endless and only limited by our knowledge and imagination.

Finally one is to ritually seal a drop of one's own blood within the bottle, though some may feel that this action is outside of their accepted beliefs and practice. For those who feel the addition of a drop of their blood is not required, I would insist they meditate deeply upon the subject prior to making that decision. The addition of one drop of our blood cultivates a pact, marriage, or synergistic bonding with the spirit in the bottle. The act symbolically links one to the *genius viridium*, allowing us to work as one.

Relate to the *genius viridum*, once the vessel is complete, as a great teacher, a great healer, a living sentient being, and guide. If one establishes a communicative level of depth with the spirit, one can learn a great deal. It may request additional plants be added to it for you to work with over time, or a great many that one already works with. It will be an intermediary in plant spirit communication, granting all plants that are added to the vessel over time its powerful voice that is now heard within the initiate to its mysteries. For the very act of creating this spirit bottle is an initiation and entrance into the green intelligence of the bioregion you are an intimate part of.

The bottle should be kept in a safe place, an altar, or a shrine dedicated to it. Candles may be burned to venerate it along with locally harvested aromatic plants. Small vials can be taken with it when wildcrafting, or performing healing work in another area. Also, work can be done to learn healing songs, rituals, or methods to evoke the plant spirits added to the bottle to aid in healing or magic directly without need of their body, i.e., the plant itself. In every respect of the word, however, it should never be treated as an object or tool that is used, or a source of power the practitioner of the green arts can wield. It should always be remembered. It should always be related to as a being of much power that is one's elder, teacher, and guide. It must be worked with and not used, or the strength of the relationship between human person and the other than human person that lives within the bottle will diminish until that sad day it leaves its house altogether. Then we will no longer hear its voice or feel its guidance, and we will have disrespected a great opportunity to be a part of the green mysteries themselves.

Plant Communication:
Two Relatively Simple Approaches

Sean Croke

Learning to communicate directly with the plants that we work with as medicine, food, or for spiritual guidance is the starting point for any magical workings involving the green path. It seems that this is being acknowledged more and more in the larger herbalist community, however the process is often presented as over-complicated or made to seem easy to learn and master—neither of which has been true in my experience. During my own process of learning this skill, I was often frustrated because it did not come easily to me, or at least I did not have the experience of the plant spirits showing up for me in a vision as a human form with vines growing out of their heads to tell me precisely what I should be doing with my life here on this planet while also physically removing my energetic blockages, etc. Many of the leading proponents of plant spirit communication seem to be the sort of people for whom visions come easily, and I felt that to really be successful in communicating with the plants I needed to have these deep, mystical visions that left no question that I was communicating with a real and sentient entity who took an interest in my spiritual evolution, or at least had some tips on how I should live my life or plant my garden. Over time I came to realize that I am simply not a vision-prone person, and also that the plants communicate in a number of ways that are more subtle, and more based in physical reality than is often portrayed. Learning this process of communication is a lifelong practice that takes years to cultivate.

Many of the works in the modern (or ancient) texts describing magical herbalism or plant spirit communication often seem to me to be over-complicated, with a focus on elaborate rituals, wordy spells, and incantations. These rituals, incantations, and highly specified practices can actually serve to place a wall between the practitioner and the plant that they are trying to work with. We humans are such an overly intellectual bunch, and being focused on the right intention or following arcane rituals from old grimoires can cause a person to get locked up in their head and too focused on doing the ritual to be able to listen deeply to what that plant has to say (if they have anything to say or are even interested in having a human come and talk with them that day). This focus on specific ritual and high spiritual pursuit can also increase the tendency to "other" plants, to focus on them as very different beings from ourselves who have mysterious wants and desires. Plant people are actually very similar to human people, and they basically have fairly simple desires. Think about meeting a human person for the first time and, as part of that process, setting up a magical circle around the both of you, chanting in Latin, and burning huge amounts of resins while walking widdershins around them. This would likely weird a person out more so than make them want to interact with you. Initial interactions are often short and sweet until you know that you have hit it off with a person, whether they are a human or a plant. Once the relationship is established you can move on to more elaborate magical workings, which can be so beautiful.

A good starting point to growing a deep relationship with

the plant people is to understand that they are actually not that different from human people, even down to the physical level. I felt a deep shift in my thinking upon reading this quote from Annie Dillard in *Pilgrim at Tinker Creek*:

> If you analyze a molecule of chlorophyll itself, what you get is one hundred thirty-six atoms of hydrogen, carbon, oxygen, and nitrogen arranged in an exact and complex relationship around a central ring. At the ring's center is a single atom of magnesium. Now: If you remove the atom of magnesium and in its exact place put an atom of iron, you get a molecule of hemoglobin. The iron atom combines with all the other atoms to make red blood.[1]

There is only a very slight difference in the ways that human and plant bodies move around energy within themselves. Remember that we are descended from the plants, they are our elders and our ancestors. In many ways we perfectly complement one another. We both breathe, have vascular systems, rely upon sunlight as our most basic source of energy, react to the world around us through motion, have neural networks, have sex, and die. Many of the chemical substances that seem to make humans and animals different from the plant world are actually found in the bodies of plants. For example, serotonin, acetylcholine, and histamine—all essential molecules that influence how the human body interacts with the world— are found in the plant known as *Urtica dioica*, or nettle. Auxin, the molecule that defines a plant's growth process, is practically identical to serotonin, a major regulator of human mood among other functions. Both of these molecules are practically identical to N,N-dimethyltryptamine, a compound found in both humans and plants with a more mysterious function.

1 Annie Dillard, *Pilgrim at Tinker Creek* (Virginia: Harper's Magazine Press, 1974), 127–28.

Thus, humans and plants have a lot in common, and it is in working with these commonalities that we can begin the process of learning to intentionally communicate with the plants.

An impressive amount of communication happens every day between human beings and the plants that we live with already. Walking down the street and catching a whiff of the blooming lilacs on the breeze, tasting a fresh blackberry off the vine, or walking into a patch of nettles with bare legs are all great examples of plant human communication through physical and chemical means. Smells are a major source of constant communication, and I like to think that the plants also catch a whiff of us as we are walking around. The fragrances that plants emit serve as chemical messengers to other plants and also to other organisms in the area, much like our own pheromones. Essential oils may be thought of as exogenous neurotransmitters, bringing information from one species to another in the larger Gaian neural network in which we are all enmeshed. It is well documented that inhaling the essential oils of many plants causes direct and noticeable changes to the nervous system and other parts of the bodies of human beings. When we eat berries we are absorbing information from that plant as well as enjoying a sweet snack. The taste of a medicinal herb, for instance, is one of the greatest ways to come to understand how that herb might affect the human organism. "Organoleptic testing" is a form of listening deeply to the message that the herb has for humanity, a message that happens to come along with the medicinal benefit that can be gained from the herb—indeed, those two things are one and the same. Plants can also tell us a lot about themselves by us simply observing the places in which they like to live, the ecological functions that they serve in the environment, and the ways in which they grow and change over the seasons.

One unique aspect of the ways that we can communicate

with plants is the ability to extract their neurotransmitters from their bodies and preserve them for later use. An example of this would be using steam distillation to capture the scent of a Douglas Fir or macerating the root of Black Cohosh in alcohol to create a tincture. This is a lucky thing for us since we can continue a conversation with plants even when they are not physically present. This is also odd in that it often involves hurting the plant, removing some of its body parts, or indeed killing the organism so that we might communicate with them at our leisure. It is therefore especially important to get to know the plants before making medicine out of them.

There are two basic paths that one can take when learning deeply about a plant: the domestic path and the wild path. I will start out with the domestic path since in some ways it is easier, and it is a way to do something helpful for the plant that you are wanting to learn about or from, since you help the plant to be born and care for it all its life.

Pick a plant that you already love, or just pick one out at random from the seed catalog or the seed rack. Growing a medicinal plant is a good idea here, or at least make sure that it is not toxic since you will be putting it into your body later. It is important to grow the plant from seed because you will automatically form a strong bond with the plants since they are effectively your babies. They need a lot of loving care when they are so young and that brings the two of you together. The plant will appreciate all of your devotion, and you will become devoted to the plant. Do some research to figure out how to best place this plant in your garden, or in a pot in your house. It is nice to plant a goodly amount of the plant so that you have lots of plant material to work with later on, but not so much that the plants become background or a chore.

Ideally, initially you just tend the plant through one growing season, watering and caring for it. No harvesting except to harvest seed to replant next year. It is nice to work with a perennial herb such as marshmallow or elecampane since they come back year after year and so your relationship grows. After you have been through a growing season together you will know the plant well, you will probably have sat with it for a long time, maybe have sung it some songs or spent time with it while you are feeling sad for comfort. The second growing season is the time to harvest and make medicine. Do some research and find out the best time to harvest, then with deep respect and love, harvest your plant. Try not to kill the plant, even if it is a root that you need for medicine, you can often harvest in such a way that the plant will live on. That is why it is nice to have many plants, so that you can take a bit from each and not kill or overwhelm any individual.

Now make as many different preparations as you can with the plant material. Dry it for teas, make a tincture, distill it for hydrosols or essential oils, take baths in the diluted tea, eat it raw, etc. The idea is that you want to get to know the many ways that you can interact with this plant as medicine and to become thoroughly saturated in the plant. Take it everyday for a week or more, sleep with it under your pillow, place some of it on your altar. During this time you should also be visiting the plants in the garden, sitting with them while you take the medicines. It can often be helpful to ingest some type of entheogenic plant while you are doing this work. They can often serve as a mediator or a bridge between the human realm and the plant realm, and will help to open you up to the plant spirits.

During this saturation period you want to pay close attention to what the plant says to you. This could take the form of noticing how it feels in your body when you ingest the plant, how your emotions change when you are sitting with the plant in your garden, how your dreams change or what messages they bring while you are working with the plant, or even visions or reveries in which the plant speaks to you with words, or appears to you in some form. It helps to talk to the plant out loud, tell it your full name, and state your intentions and desires for working with it. It is nice to tell the plant that you are on its side and will do your best to keep it safe and to help it propagate itself. When you are sitting with the plant it is important that you can reach a state of deep relaxation. It does not work very well to try and interact with a plant while you are hyped up on caffeine or stressed out after a long day at work or school.

Once you have gotten a good sense of how the plant works in your body and influences your emotions, it is helpful to then introduce the plant to other human beings you know and love, to get a sense of how universal your individual experiences with the plant are. A great way to do this is with a plant tasting. Plant tastings are a quite simple and elegant method to figure out ways to work with a plant. Very simply, a group of human beings sit in a circle, get grounded and cleared out in whatever way works best for them, pass a bottle of tincture or a cup of tea of the plant in question around, and then sit in silence after tasting the plant. During this time everyone focuses on how the plant feels to them, and then everyone shares their experiences. It is surprising how often people who have no prior knowledge of the plant or its effects have similar or identical experiences of the plant in their bodies.

Working with plants in the wild is a bit different to working with domestic plants, although the process of saturating oneself with the plant is identical. It is very important to correctly identify the plant before you ingest it as food or medicine. Just because a plant in the forest calls out to you and tells you that they are the best medicine for you does not mean that you should put them in your body without doing some research! Plants are tricksters and our minds are tricksters, and you could poison yourself. It is a nice technique, however, to go to a wild place and simply wander around waiting for a plant to call out to you. There are ways to tell which one is your plant, but they are different for different folks. Basically wander around until one looks shiny and inviting. Sit with the plant and still your mind, and make an initial introduction. Pay attention to how it grows, where it lives in the environment, what ecological niche it fills. Does this plant seem to be thriving in the environment? Ideally you come back to the plant over and over for one whole growing season, much like observing the plant in your garden, before proceeding on to the next stage, but that might not be reasonable so it is fine to go ahead with further investigations. Check in with the plant to see if it is okay for you to touch it, bearing in mind that it is tricky to get consent from a plant. If it feels right, touch the plant gently, pick a leaf and crush it between your fingers for the fragrance. If inhaling the fragrance feels nice, take a tiny bit and chew it up, just enough to get the taste, then spit it out and wash out your mouth with water. It is safe to taste most plants in this way without being poisoned even if they are toxic, but really it would be better to not taste anything until you know what it is and if it is poisonous. It is nice to make an offering to the plant, especially if you are picking it. Tobacco is traditional but most anything will do. I personally think it is lame to pick another plant that is growing nearby and give that as an offering. Coins, honey, booze, your blood or urine, or water are all nice offerings.

Hopefully you can get a sense of what the plant might be good for through direct experience before identifying it through research, but if not that is fine. Get a field guide for local plants and go about keying your plant out. If you can do this using more advanced botanical skills, so much the better, since staring at a plant with a loupe and counting pistils certainly causes you to pay deep attention to the plant. It is also fine to pick out a plant beforehand that you think will be good for you to work with, or one that you already know and admire.

Before harvesting the plant for medicine, especially if you are doing an immersion, it is very important to figure out if the plant is uncommon or threatened in your area. If it is, you should choose another plant. There are a lot of good resources for learning how to ethically harvest a plant without causing damage to the population, and ideally you will learn how to propagate the plant and cause the patch to expand. That is part of the deal that you are making. Treat the plants that you meet in the wild like you treat your precious babies in your garden, and realize that since you did not grow this plant, you need to help it to thrive in some other way. This could involve harvesting seeds and growing new plants to expand the stand or taking cuttings for the same reason. Maybe do some alteration to the surrounding environment that will help the stand to flourish. It is important to research this and to reach out to people who may be more knowledgeable than you on helping the wild stands out.

Over the course of all of these practices, the plants will start speaking to you. Indeed, they have been all along. The important part is to learn how to listen and to figure out how they are speaking to you. For some people the communication is felt as a sensation in the body, feelings of ease or un-ease, warmth or cold. Maybe they bring up old memories, maybe songs start to repeat in your head, or maybe they just speak to you in plain English or appear to you in visions (if so, you are lucky). Some people see colors or textures. Maybe you just notice that you change over time, that the plant brings you healing, and that is a fine communication in itself. Often after prolonged periods of working with a medicine, it will bring about long lasting changes in your body and personality, making it so that small doses are all that are needed in the future to get re-aligned with the plant.

After going through this process you will have a good sense of what plant communication looks like to you, and future workings of this kind will come easier and easier. Eventually the plants will start to seek you out, and you will have a group of friends with you whenever you are out in the woods. Some people find that after becoming very intimate with a plant all they have to do is call to it, and the plant will be there with them, bringing all of its healing powers with it. Working from this place of deep intimacy with the plants is a wonderful starting point for more complex magical workings or to begin learning how to heal others through herbs.

The Wisdom of the Trees

Julie Charette Nunn

Shamanic Herbalism is the oldest way of healing on our planet. In this tradition of healing, most of what is experienced is invisible. We start out in the quiet of our yards and garden, and we expand our consciousness with breath and intention into the invisible realms. It is in these realms of expansion that we may hear the voices of the plants and receive their wisdom. Here, I share a bit about my practice as a shamanic herbalist and how I came to connect so significantly with the trees. Then I share some wisdom of the trees that are my teachers and companions and, for each, a shamanic listening exercise so that you may learn the practices as well. My experience with teaching this is that even the most reluctant people have opened up when participating in these practices. There is immense joy in calling in the trees as our teachers and there is a view of a fuller life to be experienced.

Last summer, during a prosperity training in Vermont, I was given the task to sit outside in silence for twenty minutes. The wind was strong, so strong that it scared me a little. I connected with the trees, I watched them bending and swaying and noticed their resilience. Then it came over me that I so often asked the trees for wisdom, so often come to them for

45

guidance and was being selfish. Maybe, sometimes, I should just be with the trees and not talk to them or ask them for help and support. And the trees responded: "We want you to constantly be talking to us, asking for wisdom, asking for support. There are not many people that do this anymore. You must do it as much as possible". At this moment I realized that I was making myself small by thinking I should not be connecting with the trees in an expanded way all the time. I had thought I was imposing on them. I realized in that moment that what I have been given in my ability to communicate with the trees must be cultivated and shared.

As a child who spent time in the forests and parks, I played under the cedars and felt at home. The old growth of the Olympia National Forest brought me nourishment. But it would not be until mid-life that I found a place with the trees as wisdom keepers and healers of the spirit. I had gone to Lake Quinault to have a nice family outing. What I witnessed when we drove near the lake was massive clear-cutting. I was devastated. I told the trees in a silent prayer that I would return to connect with them soon, to witness what had happened to them.

I did return. I left my mom's house in my car alone, drove out of town and toward Lake Quinault. I found a dirt road around the wild side of the lake and started on it. I came to a very large, old-growth Douglas fir tree that was growing near the road. I got out of my car and immediately began to sob. I told the tree how sorry I was for all the clear-cutting that the humans were doing. I circled around the tree and cried and cried. Then I asked the tree what I could do. "Soon it will be time for the cutting of the trees to stop". It told me. "The ones that are cutting the trees will not be the ones to stop it". I knew what the tree meant. It meant that the trees would stop the clear cutting. I did not understand this but knew that this was so.

I drove around further and walked up a trail and found the largest western hemlock tree I have ever seen. Its diameter must have been six feet or more. I leaned up against this tree and began my lament again, asking for wisdom about what I can do. The energy of this tree was very happy and sweet. It basically told me, "Don't worry, be happy". Then this beautiful, expansive tree told me that it was my job to tell the stories of the trees. I now knew what was mine to do.

I began my work. My husband and I were living near a very large managed forest north of Seattle. I spent most of my days walking in the forest and connecting with the trees. I listened to them and they taught me a lot. Around this time, I began to study shamanism. In the realm of the shamanic journey, I met a shamanic herbalist, spirit teacher from a very, very old tradition in the British Isles. She too began to teach me about the wisdom of the plants. I learned very simple ways of connecting with the plants through breathing in their breath and offering my breath to them. I learned how to talk to them. The wisdom I received was immense. It was outside of my normal perception of how to live my life. I began to expand my consciousness with the help of the trees.

These practices are meant to be done with the trees that grow around us. Go right outside in your yard or garden or nearby in a park and begin your lessons. The reason this is so important is that then you create a home life of richness. You begin to create an expansive foundation for the life you are meant to live. There is no need to go to some far away place to connect with a guru or take an exotic plant to learn deeper awareness. It is so profound, the wisdom and healing of the mind and spirit that occurs, and it is so near us.

Here is a simple shamanic listening exercise to allow you to expand your consciousness into the invisible realms so that you may receive the wisdom of the trees.

Breathing the Breath of the Trees:
Shamanic Listening Exercise

Go out on the land, in your yard or to a nearby park to a tree with which you are already familiar. Walk up to the tree and bring attention to your breath. Breathe a few breaths naturally. Now put your dominant hand on the trunk of the tree and breathe, imagining the oxygen of the tree is the breath you are breathing in and as you exhale, offer your breath to the tree. Do this for twenty-one breaths. Then ask the tree, "Who am I?" and listen. Listen with more than your ears. You may hear something, see something, sense something, even smell something. When this is complete, offer gratitude to the tree.

MY TREES

Many trees are my teachers. I share four of them with you here. After a short description of my connection with each of the trees, I offer a shamanic listening exercise so that you can experience the wisdom of these trees. When you are engaged in these exercises, allow yourself to receive wisdom without taking time to analyze it. When you are complete with each exercise, you can then make notes and consider the meaning of what you received. Allow trust and willingness so that you may see through new eyes.

CEDAR

My childhood tree has become the greatest teacher here for us on our land. In one of my walks out into our upper meadow, I took time to gaze up at the very large western red cedar tree that grows near the road. I was stopped by the energy that this tree was sharing. And in an instant I sensed the holiness of cedar. I bowed my head to her, and I felt surrounded by intelligence.

Becoming Like Cedar:
Shamanic Listening Exercise

Find a cedar to which you are drawn. This will be one that you can lean your back up against. Come up to cedar and put your dominant hand on the trunk. Breathe seven breaths with cedar, imagining that the breath you breathe in is the oxygen given off by cedar and the breath you breathe out you are giving to cedar. Turn around so your back is to the tree and lean up against cedar. Imagine your feet growing roots into the earth. Imagine your legs and your torso becoming the trunk of the cedar. Imagine your arms as cedar branches, and your head is the top of the cedar tree. Breathe with this experience, again breathing in the breath of cedar and breathing out offering your breath. Now as cedar, breathe. Breathe in carbon dioxide and breathe out oxygen. Do this for at least seven breaths. And again breathe as human, breathing with cedar. When this is complete, offer gratitude. You may want to record your experience of this in a journal. As you do this exercise with cedar several times, you will become aware that you are more than the ordinary being that you thought you were.

APPLE

We have several apple trees on our land. There is one very large tree beneath which we sit when we have our classes.

When I first moved here to this land, I would go out under this tree and my hair would often get caught in the limbs hanging down. The apple was begging me to pay attention to her. I started listening and the tree taught me about self love. Many people have come to our land for classes and individual mentoring and stood under the apple tree and listened to her teachings. She is a beloved part of our family and community here at our farm.

Apple Teaches about Sweetness and Self Love:
Shamanic Listening Exercise

This exercise is best done near or on the full moon and when there are apples on the tree. Go outside and stand under your apple tree as the full moon is rising. Notice the apples and also notice that within the light of the full moon, the apples are glowing. They are golden orbs of light. Allow this to be. Do not force the image, you will see it if you allow it. As you perceive this golden light, allow it to take you inward, to a place of sweetness where there is only love. Breathe this in and allow it to fill you. Follow the pathway out again until you are under your apple tree with eyes open. Offer gratitude to the apple and the full moon for this gift. Craft your favorite apple dish. Apple sauce, apple pie, etc., or herbs infused in organic apple cider vinegar. When you are done, place this under the apple tree. (You will probably want to have some kind of protection from critters if you made a sweet apple dish). Let this sit under the apple tree in the full moon light all night long. The next day, take in the sweetness of love, eat your apple dish or if you made an herbal vinegar, you can pour just a bit in a glass of water and drink. Give thanks again for the moon, apple tree, and the sweetness of love that is always within you.

COTTONWOOD

There is a lovely park in Seattle near Lake Washington where several cottonwood trees live. In the late winter, when the leaf buds begin to swell, a resin oozes out of the buds. This sticky resin relieves pain and heals sore muscles and nerves. The cottonwood tree, says legend, was one of the ingredients in flying ointment, the salve that the witches used for their shamanic journeys. As I have worked with cottonwood, I have begun to understand why this tree was utilized for this magic. Cottonwood will take your fear and replace it with inspiration.

Fear into Inspiration with Cottonwood:
Shamanic Listening Exercise

Go in search of some cottonwood trees. They like to grow near water. Stand before the cottonwood tree and bring attention to your breath. Bow your head down and through your crown chakra, release any fears that you have, from the past or present. Give them to the cottonwood tree. Allow this until it feels complete. The cottonwood will transmute your fears, it will neutralize them with the water they contain. Now ask the cottonwood tree for inspiration to fill you. Again allow this to come through the top of your head. Allow it until this feels complete. Give thanks to the cottonwood.

HAWTHORNE

I met this tree in an herbal class by drinking an infusion of hawthorne leaf and flowers. The taste was unusual to me and rich. I decided to go out to a nearby park and harvest the leaf and flower myself so that I could continue to receive this divine nourishment. I took it home and made tincture from it, leaf and flower infused in alcohol. That night I had a dream that I had sex with a hawthorne tree. The landscape in the dream felt old, like I was experiencing a past life. I writhed on the ground in ecstatic connection to this tree. And I for the first time knew what it was like to be pansexual. As you can imagine, that dream charged my path as a shamanic herbalist.

Hawthorne is the World Tree:
Shamanic Listening Exercise

Go outside where the hawthorne grows. Imagine that you are the world tree. You are the world as hawthorne. Do not think about this too much. Just allow the intention to be there for this. Bring attention to your breath and then, with hawthorne, take three breaths, inhaling its oxygen and releasing your breath as an offering. What do you see/experience as the world, inward/outward, always connected above/below, connected in conscious creation? Breathe as hawthorne tree, as world. Go walking around outside with this same energy, breathing as hawthorne, as world, connected to inner/outer, above/below. What do you see, feel, smell, taste, hear? When this is complete, offer gratitude to hawthorne and what you witnessed and experienced.

The compassion offered by the trees has been forgotten by many people. It is from this place of separation and forgetfulness that we do things like clear-cut trees. As we remember the wisdom of the trees, we learn to love more deeply, and from this place we can help to heal our world. It is a commitment to practice these ways. It is not always easy because we can feel very alone and think that we are the only ones practicing this. It is very good to get with groups of like-minded people who are open to such ways and it is very good to find teachers to study with who can guide you as you are called deeper.

I leave you with this spirited exercise you can do with the trees to shift your perspective. For one day, ask the trees about every decision you need to make and follow it. When asking your favorite tree, breathe seven breaths with the tree, exchanging your breath and then ask each question. This could possibly change everything for you.

May it be in Beauty.

Benedicaria:

The Blessing Way of Southern Italian Folk Medicine

Gail Faith Edwards

In the remote mountain villages of Southern Italia, like ours, the old ways still thrive. We are a tribal culture, an indigenous people, descendants of the ancient Lucani Tribe; we are remembered as the People of the Sacred Wood, of the White Light. Our animal totems are the wolf and the deer. Our sacred traditions have been passed along orally, for many thousands of years.

We speak a variation of the Neapolitan dialect, use hand signals and glances, wear protective charms, and recite secret prayers that have been handed down through our family lines for generations. We pray with a string of beads called a rosary. We light candles when making offerings, petitions, prayers, and blessings. We make novenas and pilgrimages in honor of our beloved saints. We walk together in processions, singing timeless chants, led by our parish priest. We use holy water and sacred salts to sanctify and cleanse. We anoint, heal, and divine with olive oil, pressed from the fruit of our sacred tree of peace, and use a multitude of plants to bless, consecrate, and heal. These ancient ways are our treasures. They are our inheritance. They vibrate with primordial truth and intensity and exist right beside, inside, and outside of the rituals of the Catholic Church.

My rural village, Monte San Giacomo, with roots going back beyond the Neolithic, sits at the foot of the highest mountain in our area, Mont Cervati, which means *mountain of the deer*. The deer was the sacred animal of Diana, and in much earlier times this mountain was known as her holy ground, her habitat. Her ancient shrine sits atop the mountain in a grotto and people still walk to it in holy pilgrimage, every August fifth, as they have for countless centuries.

Diana is now called Our Lady of the Snow, but the old ones remember She Who Knows. Diana means *heavenly, divine*, and she is our Lady of the Moon, the huntress, guardian of the woodlands, and protector during childbirth. She is luminous, shining, and though she has been renamed, she still carries all the old iconographic associations. She is easy to recognize. She is adored as our defender, our guardian spirit, and the one from whom our sacred waters, and hence all our nourishment, flows. She is fertile, fruitful, and fecund.

Benedicaria is a relatively new word, coined in the Americas, to describe the old ways of Southern Italia spiritual culture and tradition. In the region of Campania, where my village is located, we refer to the old ways of healing, cleansing, and religious devotion as *Fa Lu Santuccio*, which literally means, "Do a little holy thing". We call a practitioner of these traditional healing ways *Benedetto* if he is a male, or *Benedetta* if she is a female—both of which mean "Blessed One". Most of the prayers used in Benedicaria are taken directly from Catholic prayer books.

Our Southern Italian family-based spiritual traditions are renowned for possessing a great deal of flexibility and fluidity. As a result, the practices found in Benedicaria vary from family to family and from individual to individual.

NOVENAS: A novena is a spiritual prayer ritual conducted for nine consecutive days or nights. We often attend novenas at church but just as often conduct our own novenas at home. Although no two novenas will be the same they do have a common thread; for instance, we usually set up an altar before performing a novena at home. The altar may be a small table or fireplace mantle, which is covered with a white cloth, often decorated with crocheted lace along the edge, according to family tradition; there will usually be one or two white or red candles lit, and the altar will hold an icon or a statue of the saint we are invoking. During the novena we recite the rosary, or offer other significant prayers daily during the nine days, to implore help, make a petition, or offer thanks for prayers realized.

INCENSE is an important part of this ritual. Many cultures around the world and throughout time have understood the importance of burning sacred herbs. There are many passages in the Bible that tell us that the smoke carries our prayers to God, or Great Spirit.

Myrrh opens the doors to the otherworld; frankincense invites angelic or heavenly protection and is especially uplifting. These two herbs are often burned together in Catholic rituals and used by practitioners of Benedicaria. Many homes have their own unique incense blend.

The blend I use is a combination of sacred herbs and trees that have special meaning to me, and that connect me to my home and my ancestors. This incense is a blend of frankincense and myrrh resins, needles and resins of pine, spruce, and fir, cedar leaves and resin, and Baltic amber resin. The incense burned during prayers, blessings, and healings is often associated with family history and carries a deep sense of place. Another incense I use is a combination of herbs I have gathered in my Mediterranean homeland. It combines olive leaves, bay, rosemary, sage, basil, and rose.

A traditional Southern Italian house blessing incense is commonly made with equal parts of camphor, myrtle leaves, and nutmeg. When doing a house blessing ritual we burn the incense, allowing the sacred smoke to flow freely as we sprinkle holy water on all corners of the house using a bunch of rue or a branch of rosemary, and pray the Our Father, Hail Mary, Glory Be and the Apostles' Creed.

The psychological aspects of healing and protection through the use of rituals, prayers, dreams, tools, hand mudras, charms, herbs and talismans represents an important aspect of traditional Southern Italian shamanism/folk medicine.

MALOCCHIO or the Evil Eye is a concern among people of Southern Italia as it is in many other geographical locations around the world. A headache or fever, with no discernible cause or reason, or a string of "bad luck" is often considered to be the result of having been subjected to the Evil Eye.

CHARMS AND AMULETS: There are many types of amulets used to protect from the Evil Eye or to attract good fortune. One common amulet is the *cornicello* or "little horn". This is a long, gently twisted horn-shaped amulet usually carved out of red coral or made from gold or silver and hung from a chain around the neck. The horn is usually hollow and therefore ready to be filled with an abundance of blessings that are being poured into one's life. The top is often decorated with a gold crown to represent success, mastery, and wealth. The blessings of this charm are many: good fortune, protection, virility, strength, success, abundance, and wealth.

When worn as jewelry it is often perceived as a badge of Napolitano cultural identity. It is also hung on rear view mirrors, often seen hanging in shop windows, carried on key rings, and printed on t-shirts. The *cornicello* is generally worn by men, because of its association with virility, but since it confers many other blessings, women sometimes wear it as well.

The origins of this charm are somewhat of a mystery. It may be Roman in origin, stemming from the myth of the cornucopia or magical horn of plenty that was carried by the Roman Goddess Abundantia, whose cornucopia produced never-ending supplies of delicious food and gold coins which she poured out generously on those who pleased her.

There is some evidence that the *cornicello*, or *cornetto* as it is also known, may come from the Etruscans as their homes would often display a bull's horn above the front door for prosperity. I often see a set of bull horns placed above the entrance door to rural homes when traveling around the countryside here. Others suggest its origins extend back to Neolithic times and perhaps even farther back than that. Ideally the *cornicello* should be received as a gift, which is thought to maximize its potential to bring luck.

In Southern Italian folk healing and herbal lore, *Ruta graveolans*, or rue, is considered a most magical and protective herb. It has many medicinal uses and is a key ingredient in any protective amulet. The cimaruta is a classic Neapolitan protective charm that suspends ancient magical and protective symbols from a triple-branched sprig of rue. It is a classic talisman for bringing abundance, beauty, and grace into one's life and ensuring the wearer protection from harm. The cimaruta is traditionally made of silver, the metal of Diana, she who was dearly beloved in this part of the world for many thousands of years.

The cimaruta falls under the category of *portafortuna* or "lucky charm", a term that can be used broadly to describe practically any amulet or talisman. The charm can be worn by women or men, but is generally deemed to be more feminine in nature.

Arcane symbols sprout from the tips of the three rue branches: a waxing crescent moon, a key, a vervain flower, a sacred heart, and a fish. The symbolism contained within the cimaruta is a blend of symbols taken from pagan, Catholic, and peasant folk magic, all of which reflect the traditional folk spirituality of Italy perfectly.

The sacred heart, the fish, and the triform nature of the branch are all Catholic symbols, representing Jesus, Christian faith, and the Trinity. In earlier times the triple branch represented the triple goddess, maiden, mother, and crone. The key and the crescent moon are early pagan symbols representing Hekate and Diana, two Goddesses especially beloved by the Southern Italic tribes, and associated with healing and magic. Rue itself is a powerful protector against malevolent forces in Italian herbal lore, as are vervain flowers, which are believed to attract good fortune.

HAND GESTURES: It is thought that ribald gestures distract an offender from the mental effort needed to successfully bestow the Evil Eye. Since one effect of this affliction is to dry up liquids, the drying of the phallus, resulting in male impotence, can be averted by seeking refuge in the moist female genitals.

Those who are not fortified with phallic charms make use of sexual hand gestures to avoid the Evil Eye. Such gestures include the sign of the fig, or *la fica*, which is a fist with the thumb pressed between the index and middle fingers, representing the phallus within the vagina. Another protective hand gesture is the *le corna*, where the fist is formed leaving the pinky and index fingers protruding. In addition to forming these phallic hand gestures, a statue of a hand in these positions, or a hand covered with magical symbols, are also carried as talismans or placed in the home.

The intentional wielder of the Evil Eye, or the *jettatore*, is often described as being especially magnetic and possessing a striking facial appearance, with high arching brows and a stark stare that leaps from black or blue eyes. But in truth, anyone can pass the Evil Eye, even unknowingly. Jealousy and envy are considered to be the main culprits and these emotions can cause health disturbances for the object of the envy. To avoid unintentionally giving the Evil Eye, many people will pass a home keeping their heads down, so as not to look too closely at unique features.

Babies, small children, and pregnant women are considered the most vulnerable. When we meet a cute little baby out on the street it is considered best not to make too much of a fuss over it, lest you offend it with the Evil Eye. One way around that is to touch the baby before departing, another is to spit on the ground as you leave, as water prevents the drying up associated with the affliction. These actions prevent the evil eye from being transmitted. Should one fall prey to the Evil Eye, we have many ways of removing the condition.

HEALING TOOLS: An assortment of magical tools are employed by Southern Italian Benedicaria practitioners and while these vary greatly depending on family traditions and specific regions, they commonly include antique keys which unite male and female energy, fiber ropes or cords to bind, knives or scissors to cut away illness, and mirrors and various weapons to reflect or scare away malevolent spirits.

My teachers taught me the use of three traditional tools to cure the Evil Eye as well as a ritual procedure for preparing them. The tools we use are a scissor, a knife, and an old fashioned key. Each of these tools is individually dropped to the floor nine times in succession to activate them, and this is done each time prior to their use.

After their activation, the tools are held in the dominant hand and placed on the head, or anywhere on the body that is in pain or discomfort. We then proceed to gently tap or stroke the area. Three times on the left, three times at the center, and three times on the right, while repeating a secret prayer. This prayer is unique to each practitioner and depends on your family tradition. It is passed along through the family line, usually by the women to a daughter, granddaughter or niece, but can also be shared with a male relative who is interested in healing. Traditionally it is shared only on two nights per year: Christmas Eve at midnight and at midnight before St. Joseph's Day, March nineteenth.

While gently tapping the tools on the body, we recite the secret prayer a total of three times. We then pray the Hail Mary (*Ave Maria*) three times, the Our Father (*Padre Nostra*) three times, and the Glory Be (*Gloria*) also three times. As I have been taught to do, I recite all of these prayers in my ancestral dialect.

EGGS: Another common healing practice is the use of eggs as a form of cleansing, healing and to remove the Evil Eye. The egg is washed, dried, and then covered in holy water, which is usually obtained from a church. The practitioner prays over the egg, saying the Apostles Creed, the Our Father, and three Hail Mary prayers. The egg is then rolled over the body of the afflicted in a loosely prescribed pattern, paying especial attention to any area of the body where pain is experienced. It is believed that the egg absorbs any sickness or negative energy. After doing this for approximately fifteen minutes, the egg is broken by throwing it in the toilet and flushing the remains. It can also be taken out of the house and buried in the ground.

The names used for healing practitioners or cunning-folk in Southern Italia vary from region to region, although such names include *praticos* (wise people), *guaritori* (healers), *fattucchiere* (fixers), and *donne che aiutano* (women who help). At times, they are referred to as *streghe* (witches), although usually only behind their backs or by those who are either skeptical of their powers or believe they deal in black magic.

Unlike in other parts of Europe, the ways of the *Benedetta* survived all through the twentieth century and into the early twenty-first century, where they appear to be alive and well. However, our culture is in a state of rapid change. Young people are leaving the remote villages to find work in other places. Many are not continuing the agricultural and pastoral traditions of their ancestors. The future is uncertain. One important note here is that throughout all of the Burning Times in Medieval Europe, not a single Benedicaria practitioner, cunning-folk or witch, was ever burned at the stake in Southern Italia.

The primary role of the Italian Benedicaria practitioner is that of a community healer, both through the wise use of natural elements and through spiritual healing. The former requires extensive knowledge of plants and herbs as well as substances obtained from animals and minerals. Spiritual healing is believed to come from an inner power, known as *la forza* (power), *la virtù* (virtue), or *il Segno* (the sign).

Practitioners of Benedicaria believe that they deal with spirit beings, both benevolent and malevolent. The later includes the unquiet dead as well as supernatural beings who are believed to cause harm to people. The benevolent beings include our ancestors, herbs, plants, trees, and mountains, the helpful dead, and our beloved saints, all of which we call upon to help defeat malevolent entities and physical illness.

The relationship between *Stregoneria* (witchcraft) and Benedicaria can be puzzling, but in their purest form the two are completely distinct. Most practitioners make use of elements from both traditions, and many practitioners were raised with or taught elements of both traditions, so much so that it has become impossible to tell where one ends and the other begins.

The practitioner of Benedicaria is generally a devout Catholic who makes no pretensions of being a witch. The relationship between Benedicaria and *Stregoneria* is complex, and in truth, a comprehensive synthesis and evolution of spirituality, mysticism, and folk healing that took place among an indigenous people across many centuries.

TRADITIONAL MEDICINE

Traditional medicine, or folk healing, comprises knowledge systems that developed over many generations within various societies before the era of modern medicine and pharmaceuticals. The World Health Organization (WHO) defines traditional medicine as "the sum total of the knowledge, skills, and practices based on the theories, beliefs, and experiences indigenous to different cultures, whether explicable or not, used in the maintenance of health as well as in the prevention, diagnosis, improvement or treatment of physical and mental illness". In the written record, the study of herbs dates back for at least 5,000 years to the ancient Sumerians who described already well-established medicinal uses for plants.

Indigenous medicine is generally transmitted orally through a community, family, and individuals until it is "collected". Within a given culture, elements of indigenous medicine knowledge may be diffusely known by many, or may be gathered and applied by those in a specific role of healer such as a Benedetta, shaman, witch, or midwife. Three factors legitimize the role of the healer—their own beliefs, the success of their actions, and the beliefs of the community.

TRADITIONAL HERBAL USE

In Southern Italian folk medicine plants are believed to posses a spiritual consciousness, what we in America refer to as the *numen* or the *genii*. They are gathered with great respect for the *genius loci* from which they come. It is this consciousness that lends its power to—and is responsible for—healings, blessings, and what we might speak of as plant magic. Many plants and trees are associated with saints for this reason. Not only are they thought to signify or represent the saint, but in many cases are considered to actually be the saint in plant form.

For instance, *Matricaria* (literally meaning dear or devoted mother) is associated with *Sant Anna* (Saint Ann), the mother of Mary. *Sant Anna* is the patroness of our village; her shrine sits on a hilltop overlooking the housetops and it is she that we pray to for all issues regarding fertility, pregnancy, childbirth, and matters involving the family.

Antibiotic garlic, well known to protect against a myriad of infectious diseases, is seen as *San Michele* (St. Michael), the protective warrior incarnate, able and willing to go to battle to defend us. My mother told me how, as a little girl, she was sent to school wearing a clove of garlic hung around her neck for protection whenever colds and especially the flu were rampant.

Hypericum is the healing spirit of *Sant Giovanni* (Saint

John the Baptist), whose feast day is celebrated at the summer solstice, when the light of the sun is at its peak. Plants gathered on the eve of his feast day, June 23, are hung in the house for the rest of the year as protection against malevolent forces.

Rosa, the quintessential flower of love long associated with Isis, Venus, and Aphrodite, is the emblem of Blessed Mother Mary, Mother of God.

What follows is a brief description of a number of common herbs and trees that are commonly used to bless, protect, and promote healing in my region of Southern Italy. This information has been gathered directly from elder people in my village and the surrounding area, from my own personal experience and research over many years, and from a recent academic study conducted by local botanists, entitled *Traditional Plant Use in the National Park of Cilento and Vallo di Diano, Campania, Southern Italy,* by Riccardo Di Novella, Nicola Di Novella, Laura De Martino, Emilia Mancini, and Vincenzo De Feo, published in the *Journal of Ethnopharmacology.*

MARSHMALLOW: *Althea officinalis*, called *Rosa ri li fuossi* and *Malva sylvestris*, known as *malva* (Malvaceae). Common mallow is an herbaceous species common throughout Southern Italy and is one of the most important medicinal species in our folk pharmacopoeia. Its use as a panacea is made clear by a local saying, *La malva, da ogni mal' ti salva* (the common mallow saves you from every disease). The aerial parts of the mallows, prepared as an infusion or decoction, are often used for their restorative properties to treat cold, flu, stomachache and colic, for the relief of menstrual cramps, and as a post-partum depurative. These plants are also used topically to relieve toothache due to dental abscess or decay, to soothe heat and diaper rash, to heal bruises and help drain boils and abscess, and against mastitis. They are also commonly used to treat a number of SSTIs (skin and soft tissue infections), most of which are typically associated with bacterial infection. In veterinary care, a decoction prepared with mallow and aerial parts of nettle is administered after cow dropping.

HOREHOUND: *Marrubium vulgare* called *maruggē* and *mentastro* (Lamiaceae). White horehound is a perennial herb native to Europe, northern Africa, and temperate Asia. Much like common mallow, white horehound is also an extremely important species in the folk pharmacopoeia of southern Italy. It, too, is considered a panacea and is associated with the following saying, A *maruggē, ognē malē struggē* (the white horehound destroys every disease). White horehound decoctions are used as an expectorant, hepatoprotective agent, and cure-all. A decoction of the aerial parts is used as a wash to treat several SSTIs, including general dermatitis, athlete's foot, boils and abscess, cysts, and warts in both humans and animals.

CHAMOMILE: *Matricaria recutita* known as *Hammamilla* (Asteraceae). German chamomile grows throughout our area and is best known for its anxiolytic and sedative properties. The leaves and flowers are commonly used as a relaxant and a sleep aid, as a wash for skin conditions such as rash, as a treatment for acne and dermatitis, and also as an eyewash for conjunctivitis. A simple tea is consumed to soothe the stomach and allay nausea. My grandmother, Maria Giuseppa Cammarano Quagliozzi, taught me that chamomile is a "cure-all" and she offered a cup of its tea to ease headache, relieve menstrual cramps, and to settle upset feelings. The aerial parts are also used as a yellow dye.

OLIVE: *Olea Europa* known as *Auliva* (Oleaceae). The olive is a relatively small evergreen tree that is extremely long-lived and a native of the Mediterranean region. It has long been a symbol of endurance, wisdom, and peace. It is believed to be the branch that was carried back to Noah's ark after the flood, and because of this is considered to speak of the renewal of life. The olive is considered a sacred tree that unites humans with the divine. Minerva taught that the oil pressed from its fruit could be burned as an offering in lamps as an act of reverence and devotion. Jesus conducted many of his sermons in the Mount of Olives, which was a sacred olive grove, and the burial grounds for many of his ancestors. On Holy Thursday Catholics participate in a special morning mass during which olive oil is consecrated. This sacred oil, called *chrism*, is often blended with other aromatics, such as sweet smelling balsam or rose oil, and used during the rest of the year as an integral part of sacramental rites; for Anointing the Sick, Reconciliation, Holy Orders, Baptism, and Confirmation. Olive oil has been used to anoint people, places, tools, and sacred objects for thousands of years and its use for ceremony, healings, and blessings stretches back for millennia. Among the people of Southern Italia it remains the preferred oil for extracting the medicinal properties of plants and also for cooking, preserving, and beautifying. The fresh leaves are prepared as a decoction to moderate high blood pressure. Modern science confirms this use and also tells us that olive leaves possess strong antiviral properties. My friend Antonietta told me that her mother would burn olive leaves and use the ash topically to cure skin infections. In Southern Italia we fill jars with freshly gathered St. John's wort leaves and flowers, called *erva ri' San Giuvanno* and *erva ri li mahari*, cover the plant with olive oil, then place it in the sun to steep for several weeks. This oil is used topically to relieve many types of aches and pains and also as a protective anointing oil when someone is passing from this life into the next.

BAY LEAVES: *Laurus nobilis L.* called *Lauro* and *Alloro* (Lauraceae). The bay tree is a lovely evergreen tree native to the Mediterranean. A decoction of the leaves is used as a gastric antispasmodic and for the relief of menstrual cramps. The leaves are made into a digestif, which is taken after meals to assist digestion. Analgesic bay leaves are infused in olive oil and applied topically for the relief of aches and pains. The fruits are heated in olive oil and used in the topical treatment of auricular inflammations (earache). The bay tree has a long history of magical/mystical use. The Sibyls burned the leaves as an incense to enhance trance and their ability to prophesize.

RUE: *Ruta graveolens* called *a'ruta* (Rutaceae). This plant is a hardy evergreen perennial, native to Italia and Southern Europe. Referred to as the *Herb of Grace*, it has long been used to sprinkle holy water and as an integral element in sacred ceremony. A sprig of rue has traditionally been carried in a little bag or worn around the neck for protection. Sometimes it is combined with a clove of garlic or a pinch of salt. One of my favorite home-made charms combines a sprig of rue, a little pinch of ash from the hearth, and a bit of hair from each family member, all kept together in a little red bag and hung in the home to bless and protect each member of the family. Rue is a potent antispasmodic, an emmenagogue, and possesses strong analgesic properties. It is infused in olive oil and applied topically as a rub for sore muscles and to relieve aches and pains. The leaves of rue and fruits of Capsicum annum are typically simmered together in olive oil; this preparation is applied topically as an antirheumatic.

ROSEMARY: *Rosmarinis officinalis* called *rosmarina* (Lamiaceae). Highly regarded as an herb of protection, rosemary grows wildly all throughout our area, both inland in the mountains and along the seacoast. It is one of the most widely used spices in Mediterranean cooking, especially with meat dishes, and is considered a cure-all. Around my village it is planted at the entrance to a home or garden as protection against negativity and harm. A sprig is often burned as incense to clear the air and at night before bed to protect against disturbing dreams.

POPPY: *Papaver rhoeas* known as *Papavero* and *papapiro* (Papaveraceae). The red petals are mucilaginous, bitter, and expectorant, and commonly prepared as a syrup that is used to alleviate cough and hoarseness and soothe a sore throat. Papavero is regarded as pain-relieving, sedative, calming, and trance-inducing and is sometimes enjoyed as a cordial. *P. rhoeas* has a long association with wheat, and the combination of the two is traditionally used as an entheogen. The red flowers thrive wildly and abundantly amidst the wheat fields here as they have for thousands of years. Their species name is Italian and comes from Rhea, the name given to the mother of the founders of Rome, Romulus and Remus. It was also a name attributed to Cybele, the Anatolian mother-goddess celebrated as Ceres among the Italic tribes. Ceres was known as Demeter among the Greeks and was the Goddess of Grain. Ancient legends tell us of Rhea (imagine red poppies here) descending on the plains near the Elysian Fields in order to console Demeter/Ceres (wheat) after Persephone/Proserpina was lost, and together they bring fertility and growth back to the earth. Ceres was often depicted holding both poppies and wheat in her hands. She was revered as the very ground from which the crops sprung. Later on, as Christianity spread through these lands, Ceres became Mary.

Datura Brugmansia Suaveolens

Um Clarão nas Matas:
Working with Plant Spirits in Brazilian Quimbanda

Jesse Hathaway Diaz

What was left was the most important element, the worldview of the Congolese that reoriented itself in this new landscape which was partly known and partly alien. As one of Bastides' informants told him when he was researching macumba in Rio de Janeiro: *we live in a new land now, we need to pay reverence to the spirits of this land.* It was this particular Congolese attitude that ensured the survival of their faith and influenced Catimbó, Candomblé, and Quimbanda in Brazil.[1]

—Nicholaj de Mattos Frisvold, *Exu & the Quimbanda of Night and Fire*, 39

Eu vi um clarão nas matas, I saw a bright flash in the woods,
E pensava que era dia, I thought it was daytime,
Era o Exu das Matas It was Exu das Matas
que fazia sua magia! performing his magic!

—Traditional *Ponto cantado* (ritual song) for Exu das Matas,
Quimbanda spirit of the Woods

Brazilian Quimbanda is a practice born of a meeting of many cultures, one that is often difficult to define outside of any one group's political or economic motivations. Intrinsic to the practice are spirit contracts and workings to persuade those

---

1 *Macumba*, a phrase used to denote "spellwork", often used in reference to Quimbanda and other African magical practices.

spirits to work to a desired end, through ritual offerings often involving trance possession.[2] A holistic concept of health is important to understand; here health describes an equilibrium of financial, spiritual, emotional, and bodily well-being—a balance that is constantly in flux and one that the spirits of Quimbanda can be enlisted to help bring to balance through the accumulation and manipulation of *força*. A Portuguese term denoting "strength, vigor, and power", *força* is used within Quimbanda to refer to that vital essence that flows through all things—called *axé*, *kalla*, and *muki* by the different nations of Candomblé and similarly by Umbanda, all of which Quimbanda is ritually linked to by common practice.[3] The degree of Quimbanda's connection to each of these practices is beyond our current aim; it is the universality of *força/axé/kalla/muki* and its cultivation and accumulations through traditional ritual praxis involving plants and the reverence for and working of those spirits found in the Forest and Jungle that guides our journey here.

Força in this context has many components, such as the intrinsic properties inherent to anything as well as subtler qualities more relevant in cultural praxis in its reference to mythic

2 The history of Quimbanda is perhaps more difficult to trace than the practice is to define. For further exploration on these difficulties and a history of Quimbanda as a separate current from Umbanda or Candomblé, see Nicholaj de Mattos Frisvold's seminal work *Exu & the Quimbanda of Night and Fire* (United Kingdom: Scarlet Imprint, 2012), 28–40.

3 *Axé* is used almost universally between all groups, although it most correctly describes the Yoruba concept here discussed, and is heavily used within the different streams of Candomblé Nago. *Kalla* is the Angolan term for the same, used within Candomblé Angola, and *muki* is the kiKongo term used within the Candomblé Bantu and some Candomblé Angola houses. Different lineages of Quimbanda will use any or all of these terms interchangeably with *força*.

expression. A given leaf has its physical characteristics, the shape and color of the leaf and flower as well as their respective chemical properties—indeed leaf, flower, and root of the same plant may have different specific *forças*, all of which inform the plant's *força* as a whole. Physical characteristics are added to by behavioral situation—how the plant grows, where it grows, what plants it grows on or near—but these same characteristics are ultimately magnified through resonance to and harmonies with other plants and spirits, as codified in various traditions and rituals. This is pervasive throughout the Afro-Brazilian religions and practices, all of which inform each other, especially with regards to plant lore. The greening power, the *força* of the forest, flows like a river to the sea, adding to the breadth and depth of *força* within Quimbanda as a whole.

The Exus and Pomba Giras of Quimbanda are themselves the *forças* of specific locations and conceptions of power, a manifestation of these intersections of power and location.[4] Spirits intrinsically bound to these crossroads, and guardians of the same, they flow with the unique qualities of each of these intersections. Many find expression and affinity in the lives of humans, and conversely, many humans bring to corporeal form a similar *força*—linking them through quality of birth, upbringing, or choice—to specific spirits. These same affinities are recognized and worked through pacts both tem-

---

4 Exu is a comprehensive term for all male spirits in Quimbanda, and Pomba Gira the name given to all females. It should not be confused for the spirits who bear these names in various permutations in the òrìṣa and *nkisi* traditions of Brazil. Quimbanda uses these names as titles within its own practices, and often the term *Seu* (Mister), *Sua* (Miss), *Dona* (Dame), and *Senhora* (Lady) are used as well for the same spirits, i.e., *Exu Lucifer* may also be called *Seu Lucifer*.

porary or permanent depending on one's level of involvement in the cult proper. As these spirits are the natural expressions of the *forças* of the natural world, the Quimbandeiro is not seeking to "elevate" them in the spiritist sense, but it is an interaction where the Quimbandeiro elevates himself with the assistance of and through tutelage by these spirits. Let the crossroads be the crossroads, to force it to be something else is a folly borne of ego and delusion. This speaks to a strong truth in Quimbanda—a brutal honesty takes shape and demons are engaged with and made allies, rather than exorcized and contained.

The power that stirs and ultimately guides the Quimbandeiro is the burning fire in the crossroads of every moment. Universally this is seen as the intersection of choice and ability, a measure of agency and free will—the scales of Saint Michael upheld on the prongs of the Devil's Trident. It is the domain of the crossroads deities Èṣù and Pambu Njila from whom the spirits of Quimbanda owe their names. It is perhaps in the synthesis here, where flame joins flame and fire becomes conscious, that we arrive at the power of the *Maioral*—the Greatest, the Supreme, and in some archaic translations the Slave-Driver—the prime *força* and potential of all Exus and Pomba Giras.

Força in Quimbanda is understood as flowing from the Maioral through the Capeta—the infernal trinity of Exu Rei Lucifer, Exu Rei Mor, and Exu Rei Sete Encruzilhadas—through the mediation of Exu Omolu and Exu Kalunga, and worked through the legions of Exus under their various commands. However, the hierarchies of man imposed upon these spirits is a fashionable construct often born of ego and projection and highly mutable, yet when we look at this as a metaphor for consciousness and action through the rituals and praxis of the cult, we see a deeper truth begin to emerge.

The flame of consciousness, that memory of light and primordial emanation in the East, is a potential—never a given. It is whim of chance or the refinement of discipline, which is the whip of the Maioral, that like a spark igniting a fire, first manifests as Exu Lucifer, harkening back to the very meaning of his name, "light bringer". This is the spark of creativity, of idea, of life, present in the world of matter. The flame is cultivated and meditated upon, transforming it into a raging inferno of knowledge—the screaming presence of Exu Mor, who is himself all things combined and the contemplation of all knowledge. Yet taking action in the world requires refinement and the limitation of this knowledge, and here it is Exu Rei Sete Encruzilhadas that assumes this mantle: the narrowing of choice and fire into a tool to wield in the world, to light the path of necessity and answer the needs of the moment. He is the King of Seven Crossroads (opportunity and freedom), but walks down one road at a time to the next necessity of choice. This trinity is the very understanding of the fire of thought, its distillation into contemplation, and coagulation into choice and action.

This seed of fire—like all seeds—must take root, and here is where the cult finds its praxis. This material world finds its fertility in the world of the Dead itself. It is the ancestors, those long dead before us, be they human, animal, or plant, whose bodies we walk upon, who give sustenance and stability. This relationship is central to Quimbanda's understanding of the world, and provides the field of working in which *força*—the strength and power to make things happen—can blossom and bear fruit.

The fertility of our work in Quimbanda is based on the stirring of two currents—Exu Omolu and Exu Kalunga—through whose mediation countless spirits find expression in the practices of the *macumbeiro*. Exu Omolu is the Quimbanda understanding of Death, itself mediated by two forces, Exu Caveira, who is the force of Bone—our mortal remains—and Exu Meia Noite, who is the Darkness of Death. These are the hands of the spirit of Death—Bone and Darkness, the soil of our working. It is Exu Kalunga, that mediator into the Kalunga itself, who adds the fertility of that vast realm like water to dry soil. The Kalunga is a difficult concept to describe, it is both cemetery/abode of the dead and ocean; the translation of the term to either is given preference by different groups and by context.[5] The Ocean of the Dead flows through all things in this world, for that which can die is part of it by sympathy. "Kalunga surrounds, Kalunga saturates, Kalunga generates, Kalunga dissipates."[6] This flowing of mortality through the world is directly linked to the ocean both by its liquid nature and the mystery and depths of those waters that contain beyond and beneath them, the memory of Arruanda. Historically the principal port of Angola through which many victims of the Maafa were torn from their homeland, it is now an idealized memory of home, the land of birth, and by extension, a name for the Otherworld, and the Shining City of the Dead. This awareness of currents, of the Kalunga that ebbs and flows through all things, is mediated by the agency of Exu Kalunga, and mixes with the dry matter of Death—Bone and Darkness—giving agency to the legions of Quimbanda to act in their various Kingdoms. The Flame of Insight finds Awareness, Awareness finds Contemplation, Contemplation finds Action, Action finds Manifestation and Fruition through the interaction of matter and its potential, like a seed buried in the earth and watered and nurtured by the light of intent.

---

5 For detailed exploration of the Kalunga from the related practice of Palo Mayombe, see Todd Ramón Ochoa, *Society of the Dead* (Berkeley: University of California Press, 2010) 1–49.

6 Todd Ramón Ochoa, *Society of the Dead*, 21.

It is in the Kingdoms that our agency comes to full use by the Quimbandeiro. These Seven Kingdoms[7] are reflexes of old domains of power once concerned with "gods" (whether òrìṣa, nkisi, or vodum[8]), but now, in the sorcerous cult of Exu and Pomba Gira, ruled by spirit Kings and Queens whose dominion over the dead of their respective kingdoms finds unique manifestation in the *mavambos*—crossroad spirits—and even *catiços* under their command. Boundaries are drawn in the world delineating these realms and while the Kingdoms encompass all nature and human domain, there is a propensity for these kingdoms to be described heavily in metaphors of the Brazilian post-colonial mind; an emphasis on the *cemitério* (the cemetery) and its components is heavily realized. Cursorily, the "natural" Kingdoms (the Beach, the Woods) are separate from the "human" Kingdoms (the Crossroads, the Lyre) and the "dead" kingdoms of the Kalunga, and the Cruzeiro. It is perhaps within the Kingdom of the Souls that we start to see the truth—for it is a Kingdom concerned with the movement of spirits, which is at once overlapping with all Kingdoms. For in truth, all Kingdoms find manifestation in all Others, and here is where the particular propensities of each Kingdom's citizens gain their power. When we begin to understand each Kingdom not as a hard fast domain of regency but rather as the interaction and prioritization of *força* to a specific end, we

---

7 The Seven Kingdoms of Exu, or *Sete Reinos de Exu*, are sometimes expanded into Nine Kingdoms. For our purposes here, it matters less the number of kingdoms and more the constancy of the inclusion of the *Reino das Matas*—the Kingdom of the Woods.

8 The names used in different Candomblé nations for the divinities: òrìṣa (alternately orixá, orisha) is Yoruba in origin and used in Candomblé Nagô; nkisi (alternately inquice and plural minkisi or inquices) is Kongolese in origin, used by Candomblé Angola and Candomblé Bantu, and vodum is the Fon/Ewe equivalent used in Candomblé Jejé.

start to see the truth, and that primal fire continues to ignite new agency.

The Kingdom known as *das Matas*, translated as both "of the Woods" and "of the Weeds", is the power and force of the Greenworld in Quimbanda. Its domain is the Forest, the Jungle—all plant life and the places plants grow—and the arsenal of practice in using the children of that kingdom: plants, animals, and all spirits found there. A distinction can be made between those plants growing outside the cemetery and those growing within—those plants inside the cemetery, while still "of the Weeds", are also heavily ruled by the *força* of the *Reino da Kalunga*, and the interaction of the two leaves those plants found therein to more specific uses. This is part of a general understanding here as well, that the places *where* something grows, indeed also *how* it grows, and *when* collected, will all factor into the potentiality—*força*—of specific powers in the Kingdom *das Matas*. It is primarily the primacy of the Forest and Jungle, and those spirits found there, to which this Kingdom truly refers.

The Forest spirits are wild, untamed, and difficult to control, often a type of spirit referred to as *pagão*—"pagan"; they are domineering and come with gnashing teeth and claws bared. While it is the "old forest"—that primeval jungle so quintessential to the identity of the Afro-Brazilian faiths—that is the dominion of this Kingdom, we find too the skin shedding mutability characteristic of Quimbanda that allows these spirits to manifest even in the cracks of the city sidewalk, which by a perseverant nature echo the strength and survival of the same greening power we seek to engage. Some argue city and garden plants have no inherent value in our cult, but it is through the intercession and interaction with the Exus and Pomba Giras that we empower all our work, and should a/the "right" ingredient be missing, they are quick to propose alternatives, local variants, and means to success in our workings.

It is in the Forest and Jungle at night, with those devils that straddle the border between cure and poison, that we find our spirit retinue. Here, the untamed ones and dwellers of the wild, the spirits of the dead who know the secrets of the Forest at night traveling in congress with what dwells there; those spirits not quite, or perhaps more than, human—for who are the Trees if not the Ancient Dead Sentinels of the Old Law of Tooth and Claw? The roots of plants that create new crossroads of life and death, manipulating the environment through interaction with it? The children of this Kingdom— the plants and even animals therein—are so intimately tied to the spirits of place, time, and affinity, that there is, for our sake, little division between plant and spirit here.

Returning to the earlier term *pagão*, there is a hint of the nature of this Kingdom of the Woods. *Pagão* as a label can be applied to many things in Quimbanda, by no means solely the denizens of the Green Kingdom. Related on one level to the progression of an individual Quimbandeiro's relationship with any specific spirit, pagão can describe this first manifestation of a spirit's power in the sorcerer's life: an unbroken horse, a lightning strike, the first flirtations of a new love interest; it is unpredictable, unstable, yet a source of tremendous power, of great force. This quality of interaction can be true for many spirits, and those spirits that retain this unpredictable nature as part of their general temperament, perhaps as properties of the specific natural manifestation of their *força*, we also deem *pagão*. Further, there is also Exu Pagão, who is his own unique identity, although his name does inform us of his known temperament. All three definitions of *pagão* are not interchangeable, but are indeed related.

The Woods themselves are never predictable, even if we

should project our own familiarity upon them. Here benign mirrors poison, and without watchful eye, talion law will show who is fit to survive and who is not. The *das Matas* kingdom echoes this very dichotomy: here *pagão* meets discernment and the *povo da Mata* become less an echo of the spiritual hierarchies imposed by man and instead honor notions of familiarity, loyalty, and exchange in communion. It is a black mirror that can be used to understand *Quimbanda de raiz* on the whole—where hierarchies appear at first universal but are quickly subjugated by the personal needs, affinities, and training of each Quimbandeiro.[9] For just as in the woods, each *macumbeiro* must walk their own path, forging alliances with the spirits they meet to affect change. Reflecting a story of the orisha Èṣù, the sickness is cured not by calling a King, but by whoever shows up with the cure. These personal alliances and affinities make the spirits of the Woods difficult to approach; they are reclusive, and care little for the ways of men. Great medicine men who trust slowly, one must earn their counsel. Here is a blurring between the *povo da mata* and the *Caboclos Quimbandeiros*, those spirits who are a harkening back to the indigenous peoples of Brazil, finding expression in Quimbanda in that *Linha*, and operate here within the Kingdom *das Matas*.[10]

9 *Quimbanda de raiz*, or Quimbanda of the Root, is the term applied to those lineages of Quimbanda that work the tradition separately and apart from Umbanda or Candomblé. Alternatively, the same is sometimes referred to as *Quimbanda de Nagô*. This term can be confusing, for *Nagô* implies Yoruba heritage, and Quimbanda is ultimately primarily of Kongolese origin. *Nagô* in this context is often said to convey a sense of "original", or "true". Both terms are used to describe the same practice.

10 *Linhas*, or Lines, are an alternate organization of the Exus based in affinities of working as opposed to "Kingdoms". The lines reflect a parallel to the organization of other spirits in Umbanda. It is these lines

Exu Rei das Matas and Pomba Gira Rainha das Matas, the King and Queen of the Kingdom of the Woods, work through the spirits of their Kingdom—the legions of Exus and Pomba Giras and their attendant spirits—manifesting the numerous qualities of *força* in this realm. This power may be viewed in terms of a delegation from those with broad authority to those with specific authority; and perhaps, additionally, to a fluidity of *força* flowing between location, time, contagious detriment or compliment, personification, spirit relationship and compatibility, cultural value and sympathy, utility of function, and personal predilection. Here is the way of Kings and Queens to those spirits under them—regents act through their legions by means of the breadth of their *força*, which circumscribes the power and authority of their "subjects". Those spirits that operate in other Kingdoms, while their *força* manifests a specific way elsewhere, within this Kingdom they manifest differently, with new obeisance and crossroads of power. It is the land that informs this shift, for the *mavambos* of Quimbanda are working through the dead of the Land, navigating in the Kalunga that ultimately permeates all. This acknowledgement is also a description of the work of decay—the realm of those spirits we call *mulambos*—whereby all bodies return to the earth itself, and inform the the *força* of the Land with the decomposition and fluids of their remains. This dynamic relationship involves not just the physical earth and those things growing or flowing from it, but the air itself—the *aires*, which contains the winds of plants, animals, and humans alike, both in breath and the decay which escapes from the dead.[11] Water

---

that reflect the syncretic hierarchies of the Grimoirum Verum, a subject of much attention and revival in interest after the publication of Jake Stratton-Kent's *True Grimoire* (United Kingdom: Scarlet Imprint, 2009).

11 *Aire* can be translated as "air" or "wind" but a proper cultural context

and air share this sympathy, our understanding of water embraces it origins in the skies above or deep underground, its collection into streams and rivers and others bodies of water, its sympathy by nature to the Kalunga itself. The enormity of circumstance and purpose that define each time and place should be considered here. This is why plants of the garden are seen as "less strong" or containing less *axé* than the plants of the forest; while it may be the same species, consider that we are harvesting *more* than just the physical properties of the plant. Every leaf of the forest contains the ground and the Dead under its roots, the *aires* and waters of its locale; the fire of its *força* is stirred by those who know through tradition or inspiration.

The nature of Exu Rei das Matas is informed by the Brazilian forests themselves, and for the reasons above, the nature of each particular jungle or forest informs how the King there manifests. Shapeshifting, mercurial, and the watcher-never-seen, he is a more distant presence, informed by the memory of òrìṣas like Òsányìn, *minkisi* such as *Katende* and *Kitembo*, and spirits like the Brazilian *Curupira* and *Ŷaci-ŷaterê*, among others.[12] An intersection of countless roads seen and un-

must also be understood. Several spiritual illnesses can be a result of these winds of decay, and the sources of these winds can be plant or animal, or even purposefully sent through sorcery; they can affect one ambiently, or purposefully, and are part of a larger conception in both indigenous and Iberian worldview.

12 *Òsányìn* is the Yoruba deity of plants and the forest, a one-legged, one-armed sorcerer of the Deep Woods. He is a profoundly mysterious *òrìṣa*, and his *axé* is necessary for the cults of all the *òrìṣas* of Candomblé Nagô—for the medicine of healing their followers as well as ritually consecrating shrines and implements: *Kò sí ewé, Kò sí Òrìṣá*. Without leaves, there are no orisha. *Katende* is the Candomblé Angola equivalent to *Òsányìn*, and while this *nkisi* (deity) has distinct ritual differences

seen, Exu Rei das Matas takes up the *opa-Òsányìn*—the seven pronged iron staff of the herbalist òrìṣa—and administers the the *axé* of the forest, through the agency and *força* of spirits in his Kingdom.

If Exu Rei das Matas is akin to *Òsányìn*, Exu das Matas—not the King—and his brethren are perhaps more similar to the Brazilian incarnation of *Òṣóòsì*, the Yoruba òrìṣa of the hunt. A tracker and warrior of the forest, *Òṣóòsì* in Brazil takes on a heavily indigenous character, a wandering medicine-man adorned in feathers and knowledgeable in all the cures and poisons the jungle provides. Where this mixes and merges with the *Tatá Ganga* and *Tatá Kisaba* of the Kongolese, the *Ialorìxá* and *Gaiaku* of Candomblé, and even the sorcerers and witches of European heresy and legend, we begin to find a demeanor and expression of the *povo de Mata* truly and uniquely Brazilian.[13] So if Exu Rei das Matas rules the Forests of Quimbanda, how do his legions express the *força* of the Woods?

---

and lore from that spirit, the Yoruba predominance in Brazil has largely blurred the two. *Kitembo* is the Candomblé Angola nkisi of the World Tree, a deity associated with air, time, and transformation, and navigation in the forest equivalent to the Yoruba *Iroko Curupira* and *Ŷaci-ŷaterê* are Brazilian folk spirits, a merging of Tupi and other indigenous spirits with European and possibly African beliefs. Both trickster spirits of the forest, they can be heavily wrathful if provoked, devouring those who take more than they need from the forest, or hunt animals who are nursing their young.

13 *Tatá Ganga*: the diviner-healer priest of the Candomble Angola and Bantu traditions, *Tatá Kisaba* are the ritual herbalists of the same; the *Ialorixás* and *Gaiakus* are the *mae-de-santos* of Candomblé—the initiated priestesses of the Yoruba and Fon-Ewe traditions more specifically. European grimoiric sorcery praxis and ideas of poisoner-witches are also of influence in the scope of how these spirits manifest.

The legions of Quimbanda are far more numerous than the scope of this exploration, but the spirits that operate in the Kingdom of the Woods bring either intense familiarity with the Woods and the unique mysteries therein, or in some cases we start to see the influence of specific plants within the Green Kingdom manifesting their *força* by informing certain Exus and Pomba Giras directly.

Exu das Matas, the Exu of the Weeds and Woods alike, is far more approachable than his King. He is found where nature retakes anything, be it an overgrown field or abandoned space gone wild, but most especially the primeval old growth jungles and forests. Knowing all the secrets of plants and trees, he is an accomplished healer although he does not give his knowledge easily. Like the Woods themselves, he can be brutal and savage, relentlessly testing the character of those who seek his aide. There are shades here of *Aroni*, the Yoruba dog-headed spirit associated with Òsányìn, who tests the mettle of the would-be herbalist, before bringing him to his master to reveal the true secrets of the Woods. The Woods are more than the plants, flowers, and trees that grow there, they are also the animals, waters, dirt, and stones there found; any physical manifestation of the greening power belongs to him. A patron of the "Green Sojourn", he is a guiding force all Quimbandeiros must come to the feet of in time.

Pomba Gira Rainha das Matas is similar in nature, although her unique *força* carries with it a great knowledge in the woods, barks, and roots of the forest, especially those of great poison or vision, such as Jurema and Cipó (Ayahuasca), and equally manifesting in the waters of the forest, with close ties to the forest nymphs and mermaids known as *Iara*. She has an intimate relationship with tree spirits and the wood nymphs that dwell there, although her nature is more quiet, almost deer-like in her demeanor—when approached cautiously and with respect for her domain, she is a most valuable guide into the heart of the forest—and back out again.

Here too is found Exu Quebra Galho, the Branch-Breaker, an Exu of small favors and a spirit that can easily lead people astray into exploring their carnal natures. For those who can temper his *força* with discipline through offering and stability in themselves, he can provide good counsel and sage advice in navigating the extremes of life, and finding (or losing) one's way in "the Woods". Exu Sete Cobras, the Spirit of Seven Vipers, is the venom of the Jungle, and in particular, the serpents found there. He may be used for protection or works of poisoning and contamination, but beware the warning given to all—his nature is his own, do not expect him to be other. If a relationship can be won with Pomba Gira das Cobras, the Viper Pomba Gira, she is a tremendous teaching spirit and mentor, and a far different manifestation of serpentine power. She is the Serpent in the Garden offering the apple of Awareness—is such freedom and choice worth the cost? Each must answer this on their own—here the observation in hindsight bears resonance to her Exu counterpart.

Exu Pantera Negra, the Black Panther Exu, walks here, the leader of the Caboclos Quimbandeiros, stalking in the forest at night, using his knowledge of the deep forest and its spirits to bring health and balance or nightmare and destruction.[14] Pomba Gira da Figueira, the Lady of the Fig Tree, is also here, tied to the mysteries of the land to induce divine or demonic madness through the mystery of Woman, bringing the poison cup of inspiration to all who seek her aide; in this aspect she heads the Pomba Giras of the Caboclos Quimbandeiros. Exu

---

14 *Caboclos* refers to those indigenous peoples of Brazil, equated with the great wisdom of the Forests and Jungles; *Caboclos Quimbandeiros* are the spirits of the same who walk and work within the Kingdoms of Exu.

Serra Negra, Black Mountain Exu, is the destructive power of nature found in earthquakes and landslides. Highly protective of the forest, he is said to walk with Curupira, the forest dwarf with backwards feet, both of whom prey on those who transgress against the laws of the Forest. He brings tremendous stability to the unstable, but his presence is also marked by great overwhelming terror. He is an extremely serious spirit coming as a caboclo finding strength in the company of the indigenous gods of the Forest. Here too is Exu Sete Cachoeiras, Exu Seven Waterfalls, a spirit who demands much of his devotees, bestowing the beauty and majesty of the waterfall, or similar upheaval and chaos.

The revered spirits who were priests of the many African traditions brought to Brazil also have a strong relationship with the Woods. Here Exu Malé, temperate advisor and expert in the building of Kongolese spirit pots, walks in tandem with Pomba Gira Angola, a spirit who comes as the quintessential *mae-de-santo* of Candomblé, able to give knowledge of all the leaves and woods of the forest for the benefit of home and temple, love and money. They are upholders of tradition and strong spirits whose knowledge of the spirits and plants of the Forest is a tremendous ally to the Quimbandeiro. The healer and *Osanyinista*—Yoruba medicine man and herbalist—known as Exu Curadôr here comes to advise any who call upon him. Through his *força* come all acts of healing, and full knowledge not only of all plants but the rituals and procedures to bring them to full effectiveness.

Exu Curadôr also ties into the force of *urtiga*, the stinging nettle. He is intimately connected to this plant as a force of primal fire manifesting in its burning but healing nature. Other spirits too find intimate connection to specific plants: Exu Pimenta, the spirit of the hot pepper, becomes the force of transformative heat and alchemy; Exu das Campinas, the

Exu of the Meadows, is alternatively known as *Seu Arruda*, Mr. Rue, and his connection to this plant as a force of strong cleansing is celebrated in every temple of Quimbanda. The stabilizing force of Exu Mangueira, the Exu of the Mango Tree, is a tremendous teaching spirit; he reveals hidden things slowly to those who understand prolonged discipline, just as the mango tree plants roots to bear fruit. Pomba Gira Dama da Noite, the Lady of the Night, is tied to the jasmine plant of the same name, whose fragrance entices and intoxicates; the plant similarly informs her *força* as she invigorates through sweetness and attraction. Pomba Gira das Rosas, the Lady of the Roses, carries too so close an affinity for this flower that an entire legion of Rose Spirits is born here, where the sharpness of the thorns and the scented blossom of the rose are equally embraced, both attracting and repelling passion.

This brings about a necessary contemplation on the nature of the plant spirits we wish to work with in Quimbanda. Although a specific plant may not manifest as a singular Exu or Pomba Gira within the cult, its spirit its very much alive and warrants respect and proper acknowledgement of its unique *força*. To harness the full *força* of any plant, we should treat the plant *as if* it is an Exu or Pomba Gira, understand its likes and dislikes, how it prefers to be gathered, what it may offer beyond its physical properties to our various endeavors, what spirits may it be allied to, those it may be at odds with.

Gathering plants themselves should be viewed as a form of communion and exchange. The Kings and Queens of each realm must be shown proper obeisance and propitiated with respect—leaving offerings and letting the sanctity and unique *força* of each Kingdom and its inhabitants guide ones actions upon ingress and egress both. In addition to the influences of time and location upon harvest, each plant's mysteries reveal both physical properties (including chemical) and sympathies with certain spirits, Kingdoms, and purposes that may be hinted at by these physical properties but compounded by cultural context, the doctrine of signatures, and direct spirit revelation. Preparation for this collection of herbal *força* begins long before the entrance into the Kindgom. Alignment with the Kingdom of the Weeds through herbal baths and fumigations for the herbalist and their tools, preparations of offerings for propitiation and exchange, and the knowledge of the *materia* to be gathered all come together here. One's own *força* can be nourished or depleted through exposure to certain actions, situations, and materia and the spirits of the same. It is through guidance and training that these particulars are learned and explored by all Quimbandeiros; for the sake of the herbalist, *licença*—license, or ritual permission—to begin these explorations into the forest must also be met with training, desire, and ability. Through nurturing the connection with one's own patron Exus and Pomba Giras, the *macumbeiro* begins to understand these journeys in a larger context relevant to the map of their path in Quimbanda.[15]

It is this trident of insight, study, and license that allows the primal *força*—that fire at the crossroads of each moment—to be harnessed through the balance of intent and knowledge. The specificity in ritual and procedure of harvesting each plant is a dynamic relationship with the spirits of lineage, Kingdom, and contract, which guides you in tandem with the plant spirits who you seek to engage. Whether gathered just before dawn when the dew is still on the leaves, or at sunset in the

---

15 It is an essential belief in Quimbanda that each person has certain spirits to whom they are uniquely bound. Cultivation of a stable relationship with one's patron spirits (which are determined and confirmed by a priest of the tradition) is the essential foundation of one's journey in the cult proper.

darkness of your own shadow, or in the dead of night at the Great Hour plucked with the left hand, all are caught in this same interplay of spiritual communication and traditional knowledge mitigated by opportunity and necessity.

Once gathered, plants are then empowered to do their work. As the qualities of each plant can be called upon for multiple purposes—to draw the *força* of Kingdom, spirit, or purpose—it is the power of the tongue which directs that *força* here through both invocation of spirits and the inherent power of creation embodied in breath, speech, and name. The Exus and Pomba Giras with whom alliances have already been secured or have agreed to take on a specific working on our behalf are called through points of power and offerings. *Pontos riscados*—drawn points—are the sigils of spirit and purpose that when ritually empowered act as the field of working and body of the spirits themselves to receive offerings and empower objects. *Pontos cantados*—sung points—are the invocation of spirit through song and breath, calling to the *bom povo de Quimbanda*, the good people of Quimbanda, to come and receive the offerings and in exchange, work on our behalf.

The offerings given both in the Kingdoms and at the *tronco* or *terreiro* are often the products of specific plants, often compounded through human innovation and used to empower our workings through their combined *força*.[16] *Dendê*, or palm oil, symbolic of blood itself, lubricates our prayers, bringing flow and momentum to our workings; it is communication. *Marafó*, usually referring to *cachaça*—the Brazilian distilled spirit made from sugar cane, but which can mean any high-proof distilled alcohol—is the stirring and expansion of *força*, dancing between its heat (strength) and coolness (through

---

16 *Tronco* or *terreiro* refer to the ritual "temple" or place of working where the implements and shrines of the Exus and Pomba Giras are kept.

evaporation). Each spirit may have preferences for certain flavorings—bitter, sweet, spicy, specific herbal affinities—which may be incorporated into their alcohol offerings. *Charuto* and *pitú*, cigar and cigarette, harness the power of tobacco, the ritual smoke of our practice; it stimulates and brings awareness, its cooling smoke scenting the air of all workings. Edible food offerings are also given: hot peppers are given to stimulate heat and *força*; corn or manioc flour is often cooked into ritual food—offerings called *padês*. These may be covered in hot peppers, onions, garlic, honey, sweet fruit, meat, and other offerings specific to a spirit or purpose, drawing upon their innate *força* to add to the effectiveness of the summoning or working. Roses themselves are always a fitting offering, especially for the Pomba Giras—the thorns are usually removed to similarly remove obstacles and pain from our lives, following the stem/road to a blossoming of beauty and richness. All workings are performed through spirit intercession, and colored by the *força* of the offerings we give, both materially and through our voice and intent.

Our plants may be prepared for inclusion in *folhas-de-pisar* (ritual strewing), *despachos* (cleansings or workings), *amaçis* (ritual baths), *defumaçãoes* (fumigations), *mirongas* (ritual powders), *patuás* (charms), or in the preparation and ritual "charge" of ritual paraphernalia, statues or *assentamentos* (ritual spirit vessels). To these ends, plants may be used fresh, dry, or incinerated and pulverized. Fresh plants, plants that still have water within them (calling to mind the connection between water and the Kalunga itself), are the best for *folhas-de-pisar* (leaves for ritual strewing), where leaves aligned to the working or spirits-to-be-called are chosen and thrown around the floor of the ritual room. As people gather and step on the leaves, the aromatic *força* of the chosen plants fills the room, attracting or banishing in turn. Similarly, fresh herbs can be employed in the ritual passes of a *despacho* (cleansing or work-ing) where bundles of the herb are swept over the body of a person or object, often in tandem with song, tobacco smoke, and sprays of alcohol, and can be accompanied by fumigations. The herbs can be used to repel certain energies and attract oth-ers, often by virtue of bitterness for the former and sweetness for the latter.

The creation of *amaçi*, or herbal waters, relies on fresh leaves ideally: after invoking the spirit of each plant and the patron Exus and Pomba Giras of the work at hand, their leaves are shredded directly in the water, allowing the life blood of these plants to mix with the waters. Often alcohol may be used as the liquid menstruum. Through further ritual action and added ingredients, these mixtures may be used to bathe items and people and bring the *força* of these plants and the spirits invoked to the working, shrine, and life of the devotee.

Dried herbs may be mixed and compounded with resins of different trees (the native copal resins as well as foreign imports such as benzoin, gum arabic, and myrrh) and mixed with animal ingredients to create *defumाçãoes*, or ritual fu-migations, where fire releases the *força* wherever the smoke travels. These can be used to great effect to change the ambi-ence of a room, whether in cleansing and banishing unwanted spirits, attracting desired spirits, or attunement to a specific working. *Mirongás*, or ritual powders, are often created by pulverizing herbs and utilizing fire to empower and reduce the herbal matter to ash in part or whole, and mixed with any number of animal and mineral ingredients similarly com-pounded, all in specific order and process through the inter-cession of certain spirits who guide the Tatá or Yayá.[17] These

17 *Tatá* or *Yayá*, the initiated priests of Quimbanda, male and female re-spectively.

powders may be used for spellwork, either to attract or expel different forces, and in the creation of *patuás* or ritual loads to be placed in statues and *assentamentos*. The specificity of these procedures are by necessity the province of the Tatá and Yayá Quimbanda; the mastery of herbal affinity with numerous other ingredients and mediated by spirit invocation being part of the greater tradition that allows the *força* of these spirits to be seated firmly enough into chosen items (now containers of their power) to affect change.

Because of the geographic unity of Brazil and Africa in pre-history, many plants that existed in Africa recognized for their medicinal and spiritual value are also found in Brazil; additionally, many cognates and close relatives were readily identified through the same criteria used in West and Central African traditions. The Yoruba, Fon, Ewe, and Kongolese herbalists that were enslaved and brought to the shores of Brazil recognized in the Forests there the same *axé, muki*, and *kalla* of their home forests, and also new, unknown *forças* in the native flora and fauna. Combining their knowledge with the herbal lore of the indigenous peoples like the Tupí and Guaraní, they expanded their herbal knowledge even further.

Ultimately, a Quimbandeiro is a *ganga* (a healer) bringing balance and equilibrium: a person in their healthy state has physical health, money, and blessings flowing into their life. All plants may be used within Quimbanda, although as a Brazilian tradition, our herbal retinue draws from European, African, and Indigenous currents. Plants are used for their physical properties (including nutritive and healing constituents) or to bring the *força* of Kingdom or Spirit through sympathy or correspondence; there is often far more flow between the two uses than may first appear.

Looking closely at the plants often grouped together in various combinations as the "Seven Protectors", we may see a mix

94

of European, African and Brazilian fauna: Arruda/rue (*Ruta graveolens*), Pimenta/hot pepper (*Capsicum spp.*), Alecrim/rosemary (*Rosmarinus officinalis*), Manjericão/basil (*Ocimum sp.*), Espada de São Jorge/mother-in-law's-tongue (*Sansevieria trifasciata/S. zeylanica*), Abre Caminho/road opener (*Lygopodium volubile*), Guiné/henweed (*Petiveria alliaceae*), Levante/spearmint (*Mentha viridis*), and Comigo Ninguém Pode/dumb cane (*Dieffenbachia pictada*).[18]

Arruda (*Ruta graveolens*), or common rue, is a most bitter plant and used heavily in European herbalism for protection, to expel negativity, and avert the Evil Eye. Using this herb under the tutelage of Exu das Campinas, a spirit intimately tied to the plant, it is said one can learn to communicate with plant spirits directly.

Pimenta (*Capsicum spp.*), or chili pepper, is the heat of Quimbanda, bringing the stinging fire of cleansing and protection to any working. Their heat stirs the spirits to work, having a natural affinity for spirits of the fire at the crossroads. Their use is essential in making *padês* for various workings, and their transformative fire can be harnessed through Exu Pimenta, who is a great alchemist and healer.

Alecrim (*Rosmarinus officinalis*), or rosemary, can alter a space to a cool alignment with the Kalunga itself, bringing rest to wayward spirits and yet still stirring the flames of desire and attraction. It is a favorite in *amaçis* and *defumaçãoes*.

Manjericão (*Ocimum spp.*), or basil, is a potent aromatic that can be used for almost all types of work; it rallies spirits to the aid of the *macumbeiro*. The stronger smelling basils are preferred, especially those with camphor, citrus, or anise notes. Dark basil cultivars like "African blue" (*O. kilimand-*

---

18 List of the Seven Protectors and alternates from Frisvold, *Exu & the Quimbanda of Night and Fire*, 84.

scharicum) and "dark opal" (*O. basilicum var. purpureum*) are especially prized. The plant adds strength to any working through its pairing with other herbs of a desired sympathy.

Espada de São Jorge (*Sansevieria trifasciata/S. zeylanica*), or mother-in-law's-tongue, is a plant of great stabilization and protection. Its blade-shaped leaves are rigid, invoking the very "Sword of Saint George" the plant is named for in Portuguese. Especially sacred to Exu Tranca Ruas, this plant is highly protective and blocks malevolent energies from returning back to the *macumbeiro*.

Abre caminho (*Lygopodium volubile*), or road opener, is an invasive fern that often overtakes any area to which it is introduced. It can incite to war or protection, calling warrior spirits to action. It can open new paths or level all in the way. It's all about how you "aim" it.

Guiné (*Petiveria alliaceae*), or henweed is a powerful expelling herb, heavily tied to the Lords of the Forest and the Caboclos Quimbandeiros and used for cleansings. Its roots and leaves have a strong garlic smell, and medicinally it has similar properties, expelling parasites and reducing inflammation. It can spoil the milk of those animals that eat it and cause miscarriage in both animals and humans in high amounts.

Levante (*Mentha viridis*), or spearmint, is said to invigorate the spirits of the Kalunga and Death, perhaps out of sympathy for its "watery" flavor. It is rubbed on tools and used to cover spirit vessels to invigorate them, kindling the cool fire of the plant to stir the dead. It similarly invigorates the living through its strong aromatic properties.

Comigo Ninguém Pode (*Dieffenbachia pictada*), or dumb cane, is a considered a quintessential Exu plant, both in Candomblé and in Quimbanda; its power lies in the poison of its leaves. While few die from its toxins outright, the unfortunate person or animal that chews its leaves will experience a painful swelling, often to the point where they are unable to speak.

The medicinal properties of these plants are universally accessible to all. The tisanes, decoctions, tinctures, and salves of herbal medicine are no different here. Rue may be used as a vermifuge, rosemary to help headaches, dry skin, and eczema. Hot peppers can be used to help with arthritis and restless leg syndrome. These benefits of chemical constituency are universal. While a Quimbandeiro may light a candle and give offerings, placing the tisane or salve upon the *ponto riscado* of a specific Exu (Exu Curadôr is always helpful here) to draw their *força* into the medicine for added strength and effectiveness, the means of extracting that initial medicine should be familiar to herbalists worldwide. While each plant has its rules for extracting those desired medicinal properties, we should consider what that "medicine" can potentially be.

Looking at the essential qualities of each plant—a repelling bitterness in Arruda, a forceful heat in Pimenta, a calming and aligning aromatic in Alecrim, a boosting and strengthening aromatic in Manjericão, a defensive stability in Espada de São Jorge, a pungent, expelling force in Guiné, a stirring of the Kalunga and invigorating aromatic in Levante, and a tongue-silencing power in Comigo Ninguém Pode—the spiritual associations of sympathy and correlation are born from the physical properties of each, whether taste and smell, physical structure, growing habits, or toxicity. They reveal to us possible uses for each of these properties, and if we inquire of our guiding Exus and Pomba Giras, manifold ways of using each, both singly and in tandem with other plants, are revealed to us.

This can take the simple form of naming the purpose of gathering seven of the nine common variants listed as "Protectors", and drying them for burning as a fumigation. Or adding them fresh to mop water. Or tying them with red and black ribbon, passing cigar smoke over them and spraying with marafó, and leaving them to Exu or Pomba Gira to "bless" them before hanging them somewhere. Or selecting certain herbs for a bath and confirming it with a specific Exu who may tell you to add three burning coals to the waters once prepared to bring "heat" to your cause. Or it could manifest in any dozens of specific ritual actions and steps to be performed under the guidance of as many spirits. It is in this mutability, this mercurial guidance from the spirits both of plant and of the Good People of Quimbanda, that we start to understand how we gather power.

There is no fixed method. There are signs, there are roads previously walked down, but in the end we all walk our path alone, even when in good company. The dead beneath our feet, Exu on our shoulders, we find new expressions and forge new paths into the Kingdoms, born of necessity, circumstance but rooted in Tradition. Quimbanda itself will always betray those it holds dear, that they may grow. One hand holds cure, the other curse, and on this burning path none are safe. It is a cult of brutal honesty. If we are anything less than honest with ourselves, these spirits will rake and tear at us until only truth remains. While the means of practicing it vary greatly within each house, it is clear that spirit respects spirit and the proof is in the success of workings and the growth of practice and character.

The herbal allies are countless, and there are as many ways of working them as there are Exus and Pomba Giras, and still magnified again by the countless needs of the living. Respect for the *força* inherent in each plant, respect for the spirits of the *Reino das Matas* that govern the Green Kingdom, respect for one's own spirits, *força*, and journey on the Path—these are the guideposts. It is the cultivation, recognition, and harnessing of the primal fire at the crossroads of each moment that brings freedom through choice and action. Here we forge and break our chains, only to re-forge, and break, again. If we are lucky, we may see the *clarão nas matas*—the flash in the woods–that we so seek; there, in the Wildwood, lost in the forest, the lightning flash of that divine spark ignites something. If we are witness to it, perhaps we too catch fire, and join Exu das Matas in making his magic.

DEUS É GRANDE, MAS O MATO É MAIOR.
GOD IS BIG, BUT THE FOREST IS BIGGER.
—Brazilian proverb

REFERENCES

Alva, Antônio de. *O Livro dos Exus: Kiumbas e Eguns*. Brazil: Editora Eco, 1967.

———. *Como desmanchar trabalhos de Quimbanda (Magia Negra)*. Brazil: Editora Eco, 1974.

Capone, Stefania. *Searching for Africa in Brazil*. Translated by Lucy Lyall Grant. Durham: Duke University Press, 2010.

Ferreira, Anthony. *Eshu-Osayin*. New York: Athelia Henrietta Press, 1999.

Frisvold, Nicholaj de Mattos. *Exu & the Quimbanda of Night and Fire*. United Kingdom: Scarlet Imprint, 2012.

———. *Kiumbanda*. Brazil: Chadezoad, 2006.

———. *Pomba Gira & the Quimbanda of Mbùmba Nzila*. United Kingdom: Scarlet Imprint, 2011.

Molina, N.A. *Feitiços de um Preto Velho Quimbandeiro*. Rio de Janeiro: Editora Espiritualista Ltda. (n/d)

———. *Na Gira dos Exu*. Rio de Janeiro: Editora Espiritualista. (n/d)

_____. *Saravá Exu*. Rio de Janeiro: Editora Espiritualista. (n/d)

_____. *Saravá Pomba Gira*. Rio de Janeiro: Editora Espiritualista. (n/d)

Ochoa, Todd Ramón. *Society of the Dead*. Berkeley: University of California Press, 2010.

Pessoa de Barros, José Flavio & Napoleão, Eduardo. *Ewé Òrìṣà*. Rio de Janeiro: Bertrand Brasil, 2003.

Voeks, Robert A. *Sacred Leaves of Candomblé*. Austin: University of Texas Press, 1997.

Wolfsbane

URUZ · ALGIZ · TIWAZ ·   SOWILO · KENAT · MANNAZ

Aconitum Lycoctonum

Dream Grass

Ryan Wazka

Satellites bursting apart
Walk Through your Dreams
Walk through the grass
Phalaris sends my love through the roots of this planet to
your eyes to dissolve in your hearts.
Count as many stars as you're able to this time.
Next chance you may be looking down.
The error is bee-coming optically saturated with divine
intervention.
The conception of perception is inception
internally; there is the intervention.
The treachery of the tricks is of the unknown side of duality
truth is hidden in.
The internal travels are seeds of future roots and bark and
fruit and twigs and branches and leaves and smells and
colors and lives lived around it and on it and within it and
above and beneath.
Time is a mechanical construct of a mechanical dimension
of 3s and cubes and distance and limits. The individual
experience is completely collective. The first time you
become a cloud you drip down to a new plane just as the eye

cried the joyous fall condensing atoms or what I perceive as atomic structure from this angle. Everyone is everything, and everything is everywhere. In the water your mother drinks her whole life, in the gleam in a father's eye, in the sadness of a presence lost, in the void of adjusting and coping. In the mass of streaming consciousness. All. At once. And never. Forever...a few times.

Waves pulse in us
Lose this world in a separate frequency
Tune out to never tune in again
I despise this captivity
I miss nights like this
When the façade's trance is just a memory
Of a program I used to rot in.

Oh how the wind blows
Oh how the wind blows
Steady

There's a moat around cloud castle
There stand throats channeling a vessel

As rotting wood absorbs moisture
It turns away from rooting in fears
The hypnagogic swing-set
The Seasons
Albeit rise of light
Shine on through an intricate screen
Outside world, air and sky
Blue to black
Internal golden bright significance
Delegating beyond harmonic symbiosis

Temporal awareness seething through sewn fabric
Moth's lighting a narrow pale place
The walls become wings and the waves
of the expanded being.

Sky blanket
Transversal latitudes of dust
Let the glacier be as is
The lion runs ahead and within.
Do not allow the code to be perceived as non-related.
A charge of duality
Merging lengths
The plus is manifesting the all and the linear is a swarm.

Standing to praise and idly glued to your seat
Watch the torment lurch into the streets
The calcified pineal releases its prisoner
Yet they never held these gems and so reset the stones to
pillars of dust
A ceiling flips inside out and we sleep under the stars
Unable to ring out a drenched mind so sit in a car
Drive to the ends of yourself
There you will discover the depths that melt
Always forming
No mastered recording
Flinging our lives further into the dragon's fire
There is no gold there is only treasure
What you'll see might disappoint
Or divided cells may become re-conjoined
Grass in the snake as another dream is conjured
Bioremediation as condensation
Drops of dew cascade inside every creek and every crack
Fortunate blessings of a reckless abandon

maintained within the atmosphere
Walking forward reaching back in time
Leading us to the same place we always get lost in
Labyrinth of illusion since indefinitely "we" have forgotten.

Sometimes when the blue grass waves at you it is inviting
you up to gaze at the halls of the temple in the sky. The grass
stands and the grass dances forming a gentle luscious tone
that only the wind can orchestrate. Birds always telling and
pointing you in more eloquent directions, singing songs
from the tree that holds the meadow, knowing your goings,
and delivering seeds ripe. Rationalize a more frequent
recognition of everyone you know and all things you see.
Those appearing before you might have grown out of one of
those seeds.

Wherever we make plans to sit and eat this meal
Let it be a sunny day
Make the world shake in its boots
All the good and bad formed as a knot
Sell the rest to shorten the ties.

Laid to rest as soon as the eyes opened
Clicked on the tube and they stared right back
Transfixed on all creation
It's life
We are.

We are more than a body with some thoughts.

A soul breathes truly immortal without any second guesses.

Break all the ice so we may swim in the sea.

The Sun is too hot, the wind is too thin.

The ripples from the nexus extend to drive further
We pretend to live and communicate
Drown us in a shallow sludge

Sending images into a black hole expecting your same face to
look at you and explain what's wrong, but what is wrong?
The feet you travel with tell no lies
Already, we are looking around for a distraction
No Silence as she sits in the room, sounding off an idea
A dream the others created isn't real, not even to them
An expectation ascended to a higher plain of disillusion
The desolation speaks for itself
Must I glue back all the buildings?
Running full circle but everything is still
No short sight this time
Everything is real
Tolerate watching the oxygen rise to the surface
Burying again in my mind
Inches closer to the scorpion
Expecting a sting
Instead the sky blossoms open
The stars pour down into consciousness
and the lungs are filled
A walk to the water yet there's nothing there to drink
Crown of another forest king

Phalaris Aquatica. Bulbous canary grass.
Mid-Day harvest. One hundred and twenty-five grams of
grass weighed fresh.

Four grams of Peganum Harmala seeds
simmered with the grass-clippings for a few
hours. Consumed on empty stomach.
Sharp clear beams of light
Grow brighter
Prisming into rainbows and pointy
peaks of pure white spectrum
You want to walk
Keep walking
Often away from urban noise
To fields and trees
An experience close to other psychoactive
compounds from entheogens
Its own experience entirely
A very relaxing way to end your day and soak
in all that the mind tried to absorb

The potential seen in mere grass opens my mind to the many
other possibilities nature has for us to unlock. It broadens my
view of what life has to teach us and what we are meant for.

Wisdoms of a power plant teacher discussed with a friend.

Tunnel vision of green
Woods as womb
Phalaris stands echoing the ailments of forest
senses where the forest does not grow
Guarding the tree towers it looks deep inside you
When winds swing through a hoop in your soul
Dancing 'til the hoop is shed and elevating
through terrestrial experiences to bring
supreme styles to the next recital.
An explosion of truth surrounds the

memories etched across your skin.
The beat carries with it the lies that lead you to choice.
A cloud confronts the Sun
Deeper green shades and forest voices collaborate,
oozing the secrets of the nefesh
Considerably inappropriate depths of
exploration for the ego; now silenced

A bright neon doorman clings his keys to his eyes
unlocking more than the drawer, decidedly scribbling
what can be found and passing a pen and paper through
the murky transgressions of relief. A violet rose grows
where nobody knows and I still mistake birds for monkeys.
Then as depleted fixations blend into expressed data
secretions, an opening is found as a bubble of oxygen
expands breathing itself within your color code and
surfacing at the completely opportune tenacity-gouged
moment in time. Grasses guide all and that is a fact.
External experiences become internal knowledge.

Phalaris, an ancient grass
Co-creator of space fungus and unveiler of future worlds
In a time before history had been recorded or conceived
The visions and untainted reaches of
imagination sprung forth from all life
Intertwining conceptions before
perception had been released
Away from the world of wonder
Data webs of affluent sculptures distilled within our minds
A fortified world detailed with splendid
clock-towers and solid facts
Incapacitating us in a jewel one day to be delivered
Returning to the river where these bones spread forth.

Grass calls out to me in the twenty-first century
Imagine others who have walked this path
in the past twenty million years
Phragmites, a dream sent
To address the
Futures
Of the soul

The machines of time
Molders of the past and present
Grinding gears inside the switches of illusion
The fragments of an intelligent parallel society
A shredded parcel fractalized inside duality
Creating a mirage of solid dimensions

A morning harvest of eight grams of fresh Phalaris
Brachystachys aerial growth simmered for a whole day on
low with two grams of Peganum Harmala seeds. The brew
did not taste bad though it burned the throat a little. Effects
came on immediately and seemed like it was the Peganum
Harmala talking. After a nice gentle high and body load were
felt for about thirty minutes, a wave of meditative trance
came over me that was something in between lethargy and
euphoria. Odd tears in the inner picture were observed,
reminiscent of oil igniting on water. Visual waves that
weaved the web of data nets around me streamed like alien
alphabets on a computer screen. When visions did suffice,
they were short lasted. This was a mild, content, enjoyable
journey into a meditative canvas. Not everyone is fixated on
ripping apart the intestines of a plant and choosing only the
parts most delectable to cultural familiarity. Maybe using
the plant as a whole or in its more organic un-extracted
form is a true commitment to the entheogenic plant source

mentioned. Concentrated extractions provide a heavier experience for some. Ingestion always lasts longer than smoking but much mental preparation must be completed before going into any consumable-DMT realm especially if working with Monoamine Oxidase Inhibitors.

To grow Phalaris is to grow your self. One must understand the enormous strength and potential of these Earth dwellers. Gratitude will suffice or surface eventually along the time-line. Resonating the right mixture of alkaloids in the right amounts may seem to be tricky if solely focused on pure DMT accumulation. Knowing that the way of the grass is available to tune you in to higher channels of ethereal frequencies will result in better worlds created by subversion.

One March morning,
I prepared a tea using four grams of Peganum harmala seeds combined with twenty-two grams of fresh aerial growth from Phalaris coerulescens. Simmered the brew for forty-five minutes before straining off and re-added plant materials with the addition of more fresh clipped P. coerulescens. Simmered down for another half hour. Began with around Five-hundred millileters of water and the plant material, ended up with about a shot-glass worth of thick liquid. Walked to the creek next to a huge field of Phalaris Arundinacea and proceeded to drink in 1...2...3 gulps! Wind picked up exceedingly as thoughts of the future of Phalaris rose to my mind. Observed nothing remarkable to note occurring in my body. Felt completely at ease and only focused on the medicine. Walked home and my life came back to realization:

This is what is happening now
So handle it now
When will you have the chance to re-live this?
The answer nobody knows
"Stay strong", the grass tells me, and
I do the best I can to listen.

Rue regenerates the soul

Peganum effects noticeable for a few hours, and anything
associated with Phalaris diminished after two hours. I
noticed more of a body load than usual. Enjoyable evening.
Positive afterglow the next day and it seems the decoction
did its job. There has been a considerable change in
Phalaris effects if brewed "Ayahuasca-style" rather than
Johnny Appleseed's quick-boil routine. More lingering in a
medicinal tone during the days after if brewed overnight.
Quick-brews seem to not pull everything in the grass,
though for beginners that may prove safest. Toxic properties
located in the grass does not seem to be the case as only
animals grazing sections in large amounts develop negative
symptoms. A new set and setting should be brought
forward, and currently that is what is happening. Certainly
Phalaris grass is not dangerous to humans if coherently
approached with safety, respect, and patience. That is a bold
statement that we need to explore to the end of our life's
age. Deaths have been reported from the non-lethal Peyote
tea (*Lophophora williamsii*) and from Psilocybin mushrooms.
Surely in the future, circumstances that will challenge the
validation of all we have come to know about entheogenic
plants and their widespread dispersal, will be designated
selectively and synchronistictally voided in a particular
location in time to diagnose the weaknesses of our liberated

environment. The choice is yours to build your own facility of skepticism and fear.

> Visions
> Become
> Eternal
> Life
> Feedback
> Antennae
> Receive

While in the San Joaquin valley in the first days of July, *Psilocybe ovoideocystidiada* were consumed on an empty stomach followed by two or three bowls of the Cannabis strain "AK-47". Memorable daze. Waded around a river and eventually head to a nature trail, which looked similar to the Australian outback. The "peak" came and subsided with visuals surfacing through the daylight and kind revealing thoughts channeled the mushroom wisdom through my soul.

> Kindness
> Energy

We began to walk back to camp slowly but surely. Along the way, glistening silvery blue *Phalaris arundinacea* was spotted amidst a thicket of shrubs and, after that, observed relatively common populations in heavily shaded parts of the stream. On the other side of the river, large Eucalypts guarded the grasses as they dream. A few handfuls were eaten fresh, and since I was dehydrated, the reed grass maintained hydration on the return walk. We came to a more rapid stint of the river where many boulders lay. Climbed atop and took in the ever-occurring ever-blossoming re-arranging planet around me. Deeper more vivid visions and information came with the wind. No one else in the group noticed anything of the sort and I attribute that to the alkaloids contained inside the Phalaris grass. Also, the colors in the visions were reminiscent of a smoked Phalaris extract from the Winter season.

Smoking seriously an estimated five milligrams of November-harvested *Phalaris arundinacea* extract with dried *P. arundinacea* foliage underneath and *Cannabis sativa* atop provided one of the more fancy deliveries of Phalaris expertise I have witnessed. First effects were immediate, not surprisingly jolting or anything, just a feeling of my soul easing itself within my vessel. Meditative "DMT-like" come-up with less body buzz than a pure extract from *Mimosa tenuiflora*. This lasted five minutes and transitioned into the torso of the trip for near fifteen minutes. Those moments in between dimensions was characterized by revelatory thoughts about spirituality and my place amongst the stars. A presence was detected and I turned my head. Effects seemed to increase with the moving of my neck and head. Deep breathing brought more of the DMT-essence but touched with uniquely Phalaris borne colors and designs. After twenty minutes, the dark, almost visionless journey, revved up to almost appear as if the room was bright and bleeding through my eyelids. I opened my eyes soon after feeling a push of small propulsion and feeling the grace of the grass gods caress all cells I inhabit. Overall body effects were relaxed, meditative, even fluffy. Visual effects were subtle but more so geared at archaic sketches blurred in the mists of time.

Smoking a *Phalaris arundinacea* extract also from November
(twenty-five milligrams and forty milligrams respectively)
during the peak of a *Psilocybe cyanescens* journey allowed
me to view the novel "clockwork elves" crawling out of my
eyes with shoots and ladders and constructing geometric
monuments that were brightly colorful as well as eccentric,
but I did not realize what that intimation could have possibly
been until after the mushroom effects wore off. Another
time-traveler who also smoked the crystalline extract
experienced heightened open and closed eye visuals and
mentioned a lost childhood memory popping into their head.

Fourty milligrams crystallized alkaloids from November-
harvested *Phalaris arundinacea* wedged between *Cannabis sp.*
and *Artemisia vulgaris* herbs elicited a smooth catalyzation
of normal sensory mechanisms. Effects noted soon after
were a body buzz with the feeling of "pineal activation" and
odd complex geometric shapes and flying visuals. With eyes
closed, visions of forests, trees, snakes, and other winding
blue, green, and red imagery danced so as the tides extend
and slither away.

Phalaris arundinacea, the reed canary grass, crowned
emperor of the Lysergic embargo.

Silent and still in the minds of the many
Swaying where the wind may blow

Digging its toes into the sands and
mulched Earth barren or rich
From sea-shore to high mountain top
Leveling the plains of agricultural lands
Returning cattle souls to the creator
Weaving a shrine of dreams
To cast over and above the heads of malice and malignancy
Extinguishing the pitch of the death drum
sacrificing the lands and peoples
The winter hag endures a starvation of light from above
Reeds return to their knees to think and
prosper from the cold migration
Extending new daggers and spears from moist crust
Holding durability through the tornado
lands or hurricane season
When the world seizes a fresh opportunity
to cease the mind's ego
Walk through the grass
Birds chirping and Sun blazing
We see a momentary shift in the stolen
salvation sought by your true eye
The Phalaris frequencies seek quenched
soil with a tamed Sun in the sky
Most regions with mild summers allow
Phalaris to meet its true form
Potent
Those with the heat gag the ground the grass walks on
Sending them on a boat down shaded
rivers and valley ravines
Coercing the reed-stands to grow by your
side is by no means a pesky task
Eager to assist and guide you
The neon green spikes arise

A gleam of white flashes and for a second you undeniably
see the fluorescence of reality dismantled to a simple
spectrum with no causal proximity. Gliding through forests,
streams, meadows, and plains; dying at sunset and dreaming
in the dawn. A dusty telescope brushed off turns out to be
an adjusting eyelid. Ecto-plasmic auras now display new
transient signals that linger long after you think they're
gone and drag you down the most incredible routes of
sheer comprehensive defiance. Grasses flowing across the
Earth since the rumbles in time, share the knowledge of the
aeons if you listen ever so slight. This invasive species yields
anyone the ability to terminate the distractions that are
simply weeds to be pulled out of your head. Earth, our Super
Organism, shivers a dying shutter; the Phalaris grass raises
its arm and asks the question, "Why this soon?"

Twenty-First Century Visionary Medicine Woman

Shonagh Home

I woke this morning awash in wonder at the extraordinary unfolding I have experienced as a result of my reverent use of the sacred mushroom. My endeavor as a shamanic woman of Celtic/Scottish/North Germanic roots is to be a voice for both the respectful use of this potently magical medicine, and for my ancestors who can be engaged through this portal. The mushroom is a profound mystery and it remains so despite the attempts of western science to dissect and categorize its components, reducing it to the sum of its parts. I can hear the mushroom laughing as I write those words. No medicine man or woman with any wisdom would dare attempt to explain its mystery. We can only treat it with the respect it deserves and hope we will be welcomed as we cross the threshold into the realms of the unseen ones.

Men and women have been working with visionary plants and fungi for untold thousands of years. Anyone familiar with the effects of these medicines can well understand why they were used ritually as a means of communing with the unseen intelligences that held the secrets of the natural world and the heavens above. Women in particular have used these visionary medicines with great skill, using their vast knowledge of herbal medicinals and poisons to create specific libations and unguents that would take the user into rarified states of consciousness. Women have long been thought of as naturally connected to the unseen worlds via their innate intuitive faculties and their ability to go into irrational states. It is no accident that many of these women became oracles and mediums. We see examples of these women in cultures all around the world, from Greece to Scandinavia, from the Yucatan to Siberia. These women functioned as shamans, priestesses, seers, oracles, alchemists, and spirit mediums, and they were regarded with great respect.

How very interesting that our entry into a new two thousand-year cycle is accompanied by a resurgence of interest in visionary substances and the revelatory practices our ancient ancestors once embraced. I see this as a response to the diminishment of our spiritual nature as our superficial culture continues to spiral downward in its ceaseless pursuit of material gratification. Meanwhile, Peru swells with westerners seeking deeper meaning through the ingestion of Ayahuasca under the auspices of a (hopefully) reputable shaman. Festivals and conferences dedicated to the exploration of visionary substances are cropping up around this country. Books and podcasts on the subject are becoming more common as increasing numbers of people seek alternative pathways for spiritual exploration, healing, and inspiration. I am sensing the ancestors of our ancestors calling us back from our collective amnesia and giving us a good "dose" of true earth medicine in an effort to call us back from potential annihilation, not only of ourselves but also of the good earth that supports us.

My first experience with the mushroom took place in the middle of the Washington rainforest where I was cradled by ancient mosses that covered everything in sight. It was close to midnight, and I fell deep into the realms while the waxing crescent moon shone brilliantly in a cloudless sky. It was then that the earth spoke to me and instructed me to cry every tear into her green embrace. That night I received a healing that has never left me. A month later I was back in that forest with the understanding that this medicine is a sacred portal into the unseen realms of nature. My second journey into the mushroom realms took me to an experience that I later discovered was an ancient shamanic practice where the spirits temporarily possess the seeker. It was as if the beings were experiencing my matrix and I was experiencing theirs. Thus began a year-long shamanic initiation of monthly medicine journeys where I ingested high doses of dried mushrooms and gave myself over to the most exquisite teachers I have ever known in this lifetime. The process was cumulative in that I was revisiting and healing old wounds that had been coloring my life, and I was seeing those events in an entirely different light. This enabled me to see what was hiding in my shadow and to address those aspects in an efficacious manner that produced in me a profound interior shift.

In addition, the nature spirits were continuing to enter me and over time they began speaking through me. Nature herself had initiated me into an ancient form of shamanic medicine work in which the medicine woman ingests a substance or libation and falls into a high trance state. In this state she communes with the unseen forces of the land that enter and speak through her, offering wise guidance and relevant information for her temple or clan. A guardian or fetch came to me on one of these journeys and introduced herself as my "medicine", saying she would work with me. She appeared as a white owl and morphed into a luminous woman of indescribable wisdom and beauty. And so through the initiatory fires of the sacred mushroom realms, coupled with the beauty of nature as my temple, I now work with the owl and other unseen spirits who inform my shamanic practice.

Little is written about this form of shamanism and our earlier writings come from men who were writing from the bias of their day. The Romanian historian and professor, Mircea Eliade, sneered at the idea of shamanic possession, seeing it as a lack of control on the part of the shaman, thereby classifying shamanic possession as illegitimate. This inability to keep one's shamanic shit together, as it were, was deemed feminine in character and was thought to be a device for women to achieve social prestige and lasting attention. Anthropologist and shamanic teacher, Michael Harner himself disapproved of trance mediumship, noting that it exemplified a lack of control over the spirits that entered the body of the shaman. Despite disapproval and ridicule from earlier recorders of these practices as well as modern perceptions, this timeless form of shamanic exploration quietly lives on today.

We live in a biosphere where communication between life forms is happening on multiple levels from sound to vision to subtle frequencies. The master intelligence behind this living temple is unfathomable. Humanity has all but lost its connection to these living intelligences, which have informed our knowledge and understanding of the natural world for millennia. Just as many of us endeavor to broach communication with nature, it stands to reason that nature may well desire to communicate with us. The very fact that nature provides us with highly specialized plants and fungi that promote the expansion of awareness and the ability to converse with unseen intelligences tells me that nature indeed seeks to communicate with humanity. Her magical devices have been placed accordingly, and it is up to the seeker to actively and intelligently engage them.

As nature has been revered far longer than it has been ignored, ceremony around the ingestion of these substances was an obvious component to the act of surrendering oneself to the plant spirits. It is through the gates of ceremony that I engage the mushroom each time I seek its counsel. As I know it to be an actual being or beings, my way of entering is always with great respect. I prefer to be outside in nature under the stars. I engage the medicine when I am called, and it is always when the planets are aligned in some significant cosmic design. I take the medicine in the evening, eating a light lunch and skipping dinner. Copal is used to walk a circle three times around my ceremonial space. There have been times on the medicine when I have looked up to see a soft, glowing, smoky dome around my ceremonial circle, receiving the message that "big sister copal" has activated her protective frequency. The nature spirits have commented that nothing gets past big sister copal without her permission. This is akin to a Native American peyote ceremony that I once attended where cedar smoke was used to clear the space and prevent any trickster spirits from crashing the event.

I smudge myself with the copal smoke and then smudge the mushrooms and any medicine objects that are with me. I hold the mushrooms to my heart and call in the beings that wish to come through. I call in my fetch, White Owl, along with the fey and other nature spirits, along with Pan, or the Green Man as he is known. I also call in the star beings who are old friends that much of humanity has long forgotten. The entire process is like preparing for a rarified event that promises guests from the farthest reaches of the realms, all of whom carry their respective magical qualities.

I am almost always with a close friend who prefers to sit and engage whatever beings come through me. Sometimes, I call a small group of trusted friends to sit in circle while I go into oracle mode. I lie down and wait for the medicine to take hold. Initially, I receive the visionary spectacle of extraordinary imagery and color and then pass into the deep realms of the felt experience. My body goes into kryas as it receives the initial currents of energy the beings ride in on. I feel a blissful sensation rise up through my spine and then it is as if I am taken off the stage of what is my body, giving it over to a new being that seeks to communicate through my physicality. Thus begins a two- to three-hour "cocktail party" as they jokingly call it, where many different beings come through to share their wisdom and enlighten us on various subjects.

I always record the experience as I have found that listening later to what came through is most illuminating. The beings possess incredible intelligence and a rapier wit, playing with words and opening us to a broader understanding of ourselves and the worlds around us, seen and unseen. Their greatest teaching for me has been the awareness of the spell casting that is all-pervasive in this societal construct in which we live. Through my repeated excursions into the mushroom realms I can now see with crystal clarity the methods of deception used against the populace. And speaking of words, one might want to look up the word "populace" in Webster's 1828 dictionary, which will offer a peek at just how the common people are perceived by those who hold the reigns of influence. I have been shown the artificial overlay that has been cast over the real world of nature and I can see the game, if you will, quite clearly. In this way I am no longer sucked into the spell of labels or titles or petty dramas that can be so seductive at times. They are simply an overlay with no actual bearing on the quality of the soul of the individual.

My journey with the mushroom has been immensely freeing, enabling me to focus on cultivating my work with far greater ease than I have had in the past. I lament the illegality of these extraordinary medicines for if they were legal I would not hesitate to make available to others the opportunity to grow exponentially with the help of an experienced guide. This is the work of the ancient medicine women, many of whom sought direct knowledge and secret wisdom for the purpose of translating that into medicine for their people. At this time of rapid global change with uncertainty on so many levels, never has there been a more important time for the medicine woman to return with her magic and her wisdom.

No teacher, book, or film could have given me what I received through my own direct experience with this ancient sacrament. In spite of our modern ways and the indoctrination that we have all received in one form or another, nature still calls us to her, ever reminding us that reality is far more vast than we have been led to believe. As convenient and fantastic as our modern technology seems to be, I am not seduced. I see nature and our own extraordinary mind/body as the ultimate technology and one that has not yet been fully realized. The industrial age rapaciously imposed itself upon the planet, plundering and poisoning under the marketing slogan of "progress". Today's technology disturbs more covertly with its radiation and EMF waves that are undermining the delicate frequencies used by migrating birds, honeybees, whales, and dolphins. One can only imagine how our cells are being affected.

It gives me hope to know that in spite of the dire state of affairs on this planet, the visionary plants and fungi are attracting growing numbers of seekers. Many of these people are earnest in their desire to shift out of their mental constructs and formulate a new paradigm that brings harmony to their lives and the lives of those around them. I am struck by the number of seekers I have met who have been called into some kind of service for the planet as a result of their psychedelic explorations. Visionary substances have long been a bridge to the sacred, and through focused use they most assuredly will impart profound insight to one who seeks with integrity. It is precisely this insight that is needed at this time. May more of those with fine minds and open hearts be empowered to call back the wisdom of the unseen ones through the sacramental use of earth's magical offerings. May the resulting wisdoms be showered upon those in need as we, the medicine folk, endeavor to birth a new paradigm of harmony, mutual respect, radiant health, and joy for all of earth's inhabitants.

FURTHER READING

Palmer, Cynthia, and Michael Horowitz, eds., *Sisters of the Extreme: Women Writing On the Drug Experience*. Park Street Press, 2000.

Schultes, Richard Evans, Albert Hofmann, and Christian Ratsch. *Plants of the Gods: Their Sacred Healing and Hallucinogenic Powers*. Rochester, VT: Healing Arts Press, 1996.

Tedlock, Barbara. *The Woman In the Shaman's Body*. New York: Bantam Dell, 2005.

The Rose in Sensorium

Catamara Rosarium

Rose—she is among the most venerated flowers of the world—standing sentinel in the heart of the garden. Possessing divine wisdom laden deep with ancient symbolism, her mysteries are infinite. She is time and eternity, life and death, resurrection, fertility, and abstinence. Inscrutable she beckons the worthy aspirant to supplicate her to unlock her opulent Arcanum. The key, shrouded within the thicket, protects her mysteries, as they are not freely given to the unversed. As within, so without, as above, so below; she is the mighty progenitor of the green arte magical. The wise know her for her powers and virtues, in rose, vine, thorn, and hip, in blessing and in bane. Each plant has unique powers and virtues associated with it. There is also a *deva* or *genii* that embodies and encompasses this Arcanum of knowledge and wisdom. Thus, when the aspirant connects with the *deva* they are able to deepen their connection with the plant, and secrets are revealed in turn. Each power and virtue can be worked with magically, psycho-spiritually, or medicinally should one wish. Here, I discuss the symbolism of the rose in mythology, alchemy; the color and number associations; techniques for connecting with the plant *deva*; and various ways in which one may work with the rose magically.

More than two hundred species of rose were known in antiquity, and from them thousands of varieties have been born. Each has a distinct energetic imprint. The wise who seek her wisdom will undoubtedly unveil her multifarious, esoteric insight. The exploration into her mysteries is about sacrifice, regeneration, and the transmutation which occurs, resulting in the alignment of heart, mind, and spirit—where fate and will merge and become one. This is the "great work", The Rosarium (rose garden), the complex labyrinth of the heart. The rose garden is depicted in alchemical drawings, illustrations, and engravings to symbolize a sacred space, an altar or chamber where the mystic marriage of the sorcerer's transmutation occurs.

The rose is an ancient symbol of secrets and is associated with workings of the heart. In observing the rose, we witness this with her rich petal labyrinth architecture that seems to be concealing a secret deep within her core. In esotericism the rose is recurrently used to symbolize secrets of the heart or conditions that shall not be spoken of, thus bestowed as an oath of silence. This apologue likely resulted from the term *sub rosa*, which means "under the rose". The tradition of hanging red roses from the ceiling during meetings symbolized secrecy or confidentiality to topics shared only with those in congregation. It was understood that anything shared "beneath the rose" pledged all present to secrecy. This practice dates back to the Roman Empire, as well as a number of hermetic organizations, secret societies, and revered alchemists known to use it during the late Middle Ages and Renaissance. The rose's connotations for secrecy are also seen in Greek mythology, where the goddess Aphrodite gave a rose to her son Eros, the god of Love. He gave the rose to Harpocrates, the god of Silence (Egyptian god Hoor, or Horus the child), to ensure his mother's imprudence was kept secret.

Rose symbolism is deeply rooted in folklore, mythology, and alchemy. The rose is the flower of the goddesses Isis, Aphrodite, and Venus, but it also symbolizes the blood of Osiris, Adonis, and Christ. There are numerous myths about the rose and how it pertains to different cultures from time immemorial. In Greek mythology Aphrodite, goddess of love, was seen as the creator of the rose. She is often depicted adorned with garlands of roses around her head or neck and at her feet. In lore, a rosebush grew within a pool of blood that had spilled from Aphrodite's slain lover Adonis. In another myth it is said the red rose gained its color after Aphrodite caught her foot on a thorn when she was with Adonis. In Roman lore, Venus and Adonis were again besotted by intense love, but Mars also desired her. The god of War decided to have his competitor, Adonis, killed. Venus, clearly upset by this, ran to warn Adonis, and hurrying to him, her foot slipped in a rose-bed, and red roses emerged wherever her blood-drops saturated the earth. In another myth Cupid knocked a bowl of wine to the ground with his wing, which was resting on a table beside Bacchus; from this a rosebush grew. Similarly in Christian lore a rose bush grew at the site of Christ's death at Golgotha. The blood of Christ is often associated with the red rose, as well as his thorns, which symbolize sacrifice; it also symbolizes the blood of Christian martyrs. In some Hindu myths it is said that Vishnu formed the Goddess Lakshmi out of 108 large and 1,008 small rose petals (alternatively described as lotus petals). Rose mythology is a vast subject, but these examples serve to hint at the range.

Many of the associations gleaned from these myths are applied to the meaning and symbolism of the rose in color and numerology, both of which should be considered when working with the rose in a magical or psycho-spiritual context. The color and numbers are indicative of the energies one wishes to invoke and embody within the operation. This can be applied using the synthesis behind color therapy, the chakra color associations, and alchemical symbolism.

The red rose symbolizes a deep expression of love, passion, vitality; devotion, sacrifice, blood of life; solar, masculine, or active energy; intimacy, courage, and respect. The white rose is associated with birth and is the symbol of virginity and innocence. It symbolizes purity, acceptance, chastity, perfection, reverence, unconditional love, feminine or passive energies, initiation, and new beginnings. In alchemy the red and white rose symbolize the Red King and White Queen archetypes. The solar (Sulfur) and lunar (Salt) principals, which when joined together in alchemical marriage (*conjunctio*) give birth to the Philosopher's child (Mercury). The whole, now birthed from the union of "I and You", transmute into a new existence or state of being. Thus red roses are associated with the red phases of alchemical work (*rubedo*) and white roses are associated with the white phase (*albedo*).

The yellow rose has lore that lends meaning to that which expresses jealousy, infidelity, or finishing of love. This is based on a legend where Mohammed was tormented by the idea that his wife was cheating on him. He invoked the archangel Gabriel for assistance, who suggested that when he saw his wife next, he should command her to drop whatever she is holding into the water. When Mohammed returned home from battle he gave his wife a bouquet of red roses and then demanded she drop them into the water. As the roses merged with the water, they turned from red to saffron yellow. Newer associations have been given to symbolize camaraderie and friendship, joy, security, protection against envious lovers, and mature love. In alchemy, the use of a single gilded rose is a symbol of completion of the great work, completion, and perfection of oneself. It signifies the successful marriage of opposites to produce the "golden child", the perfected essence of King and Queen in union. This differs from the use of the yellow rose and should be noted.

The lavender roses symbolize mystery as they are the closest to the unattainable blue rose, and the pink rose represents gentleness, softness, gratitude, honor, and friendship. Blue and black roses are not true rose colors but may be attained through the withering of red and lavender rose petals, or very dark red roses. Withered rose petals symbolize death, depression, love lost or ended, decay, the ending of life, and convey the death of a feeling or idea.

Numerologically, the single red rose represents the mystic self/center, the microcosm and heart of one's true nature. A single white rose and a single red rose together symbolize the spirit and soul anew, of complete surrender and permanent transmutation. In Freemasonry, three roses are symbolic of their guiding principles, love, life, and light. The number five and seven are most commonly associated with the rose. The wild rose has five petals on it and the total petals repeat in multiples of five. The number five corresponds to the pentagram, representing the four elements of matter (earth, air, fire, water) and the fifth element, the quintessential spirit, the heart and the life force. The human star (the body) can be juxtaposed over the pentagram with head and four limbs at the points of the pentagram. Simply speaking, it represents man as microcosm, symbolizing our place in the macrocosm—as above, so below. The number five corresponds to the five senses and correlates to the rose by representing self-awareness by developing the senses. In Christianity the five-petalled rose signifies the five wounds of Christ.

The seven-petalled rose represents the spiritual in the number three and the material in the number four, and three plus four equals seven, the symbol of totality, the creation in which man evolves. Also prominent in esoteric studies we witness seven planets, seven days of the week, seven notes in the musical scale, the seven directions of space, the seven directions of perfection, each phase of the moon last approximately seven days and our bodies completely regenerate cells in seven year cycles. There are seven candles on the Jewish Menorah, which symbolize creation. In Christianity seven words of Jesus were pronounced on the cross, we also see the seven deadly sins and the seven demons that came out of Mary Magdalene, the number seven also symbolizes punishment, purification, and penitence. In ancient Egypt there were seven paths to heaven and seven heavenly cows; Osiris led his father through seven halls of the underworld. In Pythagorean numerology the number seven is iconic of perfection in the specific unfolding of the universe and human understanding. It is the symbol of eternal life for the Egyptians, which symbolize a complete cycle of dynamic perfection. These examples merely name a few.

We see the seven-petalled rose in alchemy stand either alone or as a seven-petalled rose with multiples of seven petals circumambulating the initial seven petals at the center, seven times. This is best depicted in the engraving "DAT ROSA MEL APIBUS", or "The Rose Gives the Bees Honey" by Johann Thedore deBry (d. 1598) where it has seven-fold symmetry, seven layers of petals and its stem is rendered in the shape of the cross. The rose in this etching depicts the number seven squared, which equals forty-nine, the composite number of the magic square of Venus, the Greek equivalent to Aphrodite, goddess of Love.

Commentaring on this image, John Eberly writes:

This image of the *Rosa Mundi*, or *Rota Mundi*, is the solar wheel of Apollo, the Lord of movement, of the ever passing/present moment. It is the Solar Citadel, the abode of the Heart, the symbolic center of the Supreme Center which is everywhere centered at once. It is a door through which this invisible place may be accessed by one with a pure heart and an unblemished soul. If one gains access to the center of the rose, it speaks the "lost word" of Masonic lore, the Master Word which throws open the lodge doors of every sacred society.

In DAT ROSA MEL APIBUS the Solar Rose represents the labyrinth, the path and pilgrimage of a particular lifetime. The journey into the center can be thorny, but the destination is sweet, like honey to the bee.[1]

As one can ascertain thus far, the symbolism of the rose is infinite. Discerning this information can be an important basis to assist the aspirant to achieve results within one's magi-

1 John Eberly, "Commentary on *Dat Rosa Mel Apibus*", http://www.eso-teric.msu.edu/Eberly/CommentaryDR.htm [Accessed 5/5/15]

cal praxis. One can work from a strictly symbolic standpoint, or one can choose to work in an intimate and communicative relationship with the *genii* of the rose itself. Allowing it to guide ones magical praxis in the green arte.

The *pharmakuetē*, hedgewitch, rootworker, wortcunner, and alchemist whose focus is working in the plant realm is wise to know and understand the anatomy of the plant in all seasons, under the light of the sun and dark of the moon. Here you will experience the gross and subtle energies of the plant through birth, life, death, and resurrection. Commune with the natural rhythms of the wheel of the year, phases of the moon, waking and sleeping, with each part of the plant vibrating at different frequencies, more potent than the other. When possible it is best to have a garden of your own, access to a nearby forest, or arboretum. Having live flora to commune with is best and integral to connecting with the plant *devas*.

A simple yet effective way to commune with a plant spirit is by using the senses of the five-petalled rose. This concept is achieved by connecting with the *deva* in oneiric, intuitive, and psychic levels, not one of linear thought. This practice can be applied with any plant with which you wish to commune. The following example establishes the rose as the intention. The goal of this ritual is to allow the self to connect to the whole by using all of the senses. In doing so one's consciousness shifts to a realm where the aspirant can see in between time and space, beyond the veil. Thus the communion with plant spirits becomes more visceral; psychic abilities are enhanced as well.

THE POWERS AND VIRTUES OF ROSE IN SENSORIUM

Prepare a philtre, menstrum, or cordial containing rose, from which you may imbibe as a ritual sacrament. This may simply be accomplished by immersing rose petals into a white or red wine three days prior, allowing the spirit of the wine to extract the spirit of rose. The number of petals is not important but often times the number thirty-seven is used in this work.

Be sure to stir or shake the menstrum daily in preparation. Filter the wine into your ritual cup and imbibe in the sacrament as you begin. If possible, have a live rosebush present, or a long-stemmed rose with thorns. Pluck a thorn from a flower stem; prick the index finger on the dominating hand and give three drops of blood to the crown of the rosebush (where roots meet the earth). Offer a small portion of the prepared rose menstrum by pouring it at the crown as well. Set a quill and your magical journal beside you. Invite the spirit of rose into the circle of art magical using the invocation of your formulation.

Imbibe once again the rose sacrament. Ground, center, and breathe deeply into the earth imagining yourself as a sentinel rosebush amongst many others in the heart of the Rosarium. Witness that which is above and that which is below, that which is within and that which is without. Continue to breathe and align yourself with your heart and true will. Allow yourself to exist between the veil in a time where there is no time or boundaries.

Take a rose from the bush and hold it at your third eye, meditate upon it with your open eye of dreaming. Then hold the rose in your view. Gaze upon it while shifting vision until the essence of the rose, the *deva*, is in sight. Allow your eyes to see beyond the corporeal. Scribe any oracles, visions, or words the *deva* of the rose communicates to you. Try not to overthink any of the symbols or words received.

Next, in lotus posture, peel the petals from the rose and cup in both of your hands near Svadhisthana, the second chakra (located in the pelvic area of the body below the navel). Close your eyes and focus on breath meditating and communing with the petals through touch, feel the sensations and feelings brought upon by rose, allow your skin to communicate with the *deva* rather than projecting upon it the normal corporeal ways we perceive kinesthetic awareness. Repeat with thorn, stem, and leaf. Scribe any oracles, visions, or words the rose communicates to you during this time.

Next bring your focus to your nose and imagine breath moving in and out of this area. Imagine what this sensation would look like if your eyes could visually perceive the breath. Once the tip of your nose starts to tingle or buzz, bring the petals to the nose and focus upon its scent. Try to let go of any preconceived ideas of what the sense of smell is like when actually smelling something. Allow the whole of your body to embody the rose's intelligence by smelling the rose. Rub the petals between your fingers or scratch the backside of a petal to release their petals aromatic qualities, listen for any messages from rose, and scribe in your journal.

Next bring the breathing into and out of the space between the tip of your tongue and the center two upper and lower teeth. Place your tongue there and wait for a tingling sensation. Take a petal from the rose and chew between those front four teeth and tongue-tip. Do not swallow; keep chewing. Allow the spirit of rose to envelope your body, connecting on a cellular level through the saliva. Note any messages given to you by the rose. Focus on thoughts that arise as a result from the taste of the rose, refrain from the visceral reaction you may have from the actual taste. Scribe any messages, oracles, or images received in your journal.

Next return to breath and establish a rhythm focusing on ears. Imagine taking breath in and out of the ears. Once a tingling sensation occurs in your ears raise the cupped petals to your ears and listen. Note any messages revealed to you by the voice of the rose. Lastly, lift the ritual cup to your heart, then to your third eye, and then raise to spirit stating "My heart, My mind, My Spirit are One". Give one last offering to the crown and finish the ritual sacrament. Remain sitting with rose a while longer and open yourself up completely to her wisdom. Allow her spirit to enter your body completely. Find a place in your garden to plant your rose. If this is not possible find a suitable place for it to reside within a pot. Commune and visit in adoration regularly. The meditation and continued offering of blood will allow you to further attune with her spirit. Imbibe her essence just prior to slumber; she will visit you in the oneiric realms.

The following words were scribed in result of the aforementioned ritual on the third of March, 2008.

The Powers and Virtues of the Rose in Sensorium

~The Open I of Dreaming (Sight)~
Emanating Green light of shadow
The divine mystic lies before you,
Two eyes beneath the veil, a tunnel to the arcane
Blood wept, dew speaks
The spiral tunnel reveals
Arbor Inscrutable

~In Sacred Sensorium of Touch~
Sensual, wet, stimulates saliva
Activates, enlivens, glowing dew
Pureness in holy unity
Protectress Vessel
Heart pollinates bounty
Strength, Courage, bough and strife
The Sepal pentacle of five

In thorn, protection, bane, blood by life
Sacrifice

~In Sacred Sensorium of Aroma~
Sacred Light of the Hortus Arcane
Divulge to you in friend or foe
The Sacred heart—majesty and honor
Heart Inscrutable manifest at the altar
In Harmony with death, imperfection
Beyond the Black Seas—in infinite fortification
Bound by Love, Lust, the Heavens and Earth Twine
Merging the Mysteries in to One

~In Sacred Sensorium of Taste~
Arcane Flora, bitter, soft and sweet
The Elixir, timeless, bounty
Endeavor to be One
Open the Petals, Submissive to the garden's delight
Heart is bitter, leaf sweet

~In Sacred Sensorium of Sound~
Endeavor the Mysteries, Warmth emanates the ear
Breathes Essence of Wind and Wisdom—
Sings back in admiration the song of the Rose.

As herbalists work from a medicinal and sometimes energetic stance using the anatomy of a plant, the witch does the same but from a more symbolic and sometimes paradoxical viewpoint. The seed of the rose is found within the fruit (rose hip) and may be worked with in the creation of charms and mojo bags to bring forth fertility and the birthing of any new endeavor. The fruit of the rose is her 'hip', and may be employed for any endeavors to conjure completion and fortification.

Here we may look to how it is used to make herbal medicine; its healing constituents for inspiration on making poultices, decoctions, and philtres of the arte magical. The hips could be used in the creation of ritual adornment and regalia, charms, and would be a fine choice for the creation of a ritual mala or rosary.

Fresh (preferred) or dried rose petals may be used to create any manner of philtre, wine, cordial, mojo bags, spiritual baths and washes, talismans, poppets, oils, perfumes, or incense for magical ordeals concerning attraction, beauty, allure, and as an offering unto spirits in love or devotion. Freshly collected morning dew from the petals may be collected over time and imbibed to instill tranquility within one's spirit. In the matter concerning philtres, fresh petals may be collected mid-morning and sealed into a spirit bottle with distilled spirits and in three weeks' time will create an exemplary tincture.

There are many varieties of rose, some of which have a vine. The vine of the rose may be employed in any operation to bind or entangle, thus calculated by the aspirant according to the outcome demanded. Excellent examples would be in binding one to another in love or in bane, to entangle or estrange.

The thorn may be used in cursing or in protection, as well as enlightenment. Symbolically they represent boundaries, protection, sacrifice, initiation, and transformation. They are symbols of challenge, and sacrifice to achieve great transformation. The wayfarer may stumble upon a thicket of rose abundant in vine and twisted, thorn-laden branches when journeying through wild areas or the woods. The thicket of rose is symbolic of an entrance into other realms. It serves as sentinel to protect these realms from the uninitiatied—only the worthy aspirant, aware of the challenges ahead in the great work, is invited. Thickets are also mazes, which depending on the journeyman, may give one a sense of confusion or being lost. In the same way the thorn or thicket may be employed unto the circle of arte.

An old growth rose tree may be indicated by a thicket, where the aspirant might find an erect trunk that possesses a hard wood, with deep, rich, red color. This will make for an exceptional wand that may serve as a conduit for summoning and sending forth power. The innermost part of the branch or trunk will be soft, therefore it is also a fine selection for the construction of a spirit vessel or receptacle. In this way it might serve to house thorns or petals or as a talisman.

The root of a plant connects the living with the dead and may be employed to conjure the ancestral power of those who passed so they may assist in your operation. Let this be done using the root clusters of the rose to bless or to curse, in matters of the heart and love.

In order to work with rose to abounding potential it is important to understand the archetypal signature of rose and to commune with its *deva* frequently. To achieve this one must refrain from preconceived notions and cultural connections to rose and become a vessel for her spirit. As one can see, the number of qualities the rose can lend to one's magical workings as a practitioner of the green arte is nearly as infinite as the lore and symbolic attributes of the rose itself. To know her and grow with her is to Bloom True in the Garden of the Abyss.

REFERENCES

Anon. "Properties of the Number 7" from http://www.ridingthebeast.com/numbers/nu7.php [Accessed 5/2/15]
Anon. "The Rose in Myths & Legends" from http://www.ludwigsroses.co.za/literature/the-rose-in-myths-legends/

[Accessed 5/5/15]

Anon. "Alchemy Guild–Guild Rose Symbol" from http://alchemyguild.memberlodge.org/page-311919 [Accessed 5/5/15]

Beyerl, Paul. *A Compendium of Herbal Magick*. Custer, WA: Phoenix Pub., 1998.

Burgess, Isla. *Weeds Heal: A Working Herbal*. Cambridge, NZ: Viriditas Pub., 1998.

Eberly, John. "Commentary on *Dat Rosa Mel Apibus*" http://www.esoteric.msu.edu/Eberly/CommentaryDR.htm [Accessed 5/5/15]

Grimassi, Raven. Grimoire of the Thorn-blooded Witch: Mastering the Five Arts of Old World Witchery. San Francisco: Weiser, 2014.

Schulke, Daniel. *Viridarium Umbris: The Pleasure Garden of Shadows*. California: Xoanon, 2005.

Smith, Patrick, trans. *The Rosary of the Philosophers; Being the Rosarium Philosophorum*. Sequim, WA: Holmes Pub Group, 2003.

A natural born scientist, ROBERT ALLEN BARTLETT's interest in geology and the sciences in general prompted him to construct his own home laboratory when only nine years old. Bartlett's interest in the ancient use of natural materials led him to the study of alchemical works at the age of twelve, and it has become his lifelong passion. In 1974, he left San Jose State University to pursue an intensive course of alchemical study at the Paracelsus Research Society (later Paracelsus College) under the guidance of Dr. Albert Riedel (Frater Albertus). In 1979, he received his BS in chemistry and immediately began work at Paracelsus Laboratories as Chief Chemist. Working closely with Frater Albertus, Bartlett developed a wide range of mineral and metallic preparations following western and eastern alchemical traditions for applications in alternative health care. He currently lives with his wife and two daughters in the Pacific Northwest, where he has been teaching classes and giving workshops on practical alchemy since 2002. He is an instructor with Flamel College, and produces a line of spagyric and homeopathic cell salts under the Terra Vitae label. Bartlett has authored the books, *Real Alchemy: A Primer of Practical Alchemy* and *The Way of the Crucible*. He lectures and gives classes around the Seattle area, and is an Adept member of the International Alchemy Guild, preserving Alchemical Knowledge since the sixteenth century.

SEAN CROKE is a wildcrafter, medicine maker, and gardener who has been working with the plants of the Pacific Northwest for ten years. He is a co-founder of Understory Apothecary, which produces small batch tinctures of local herbs and provides fresh harvested herbs to medicine makers. Croke is also involved in Cascadia Terroir which produces essential oils from native plants. He has also recently co-founded The Hawthorne School of Plant Medicine. He graduated from The Evergreen State College with a BA/BS where he focused on Ethnobotany and Organic Chemistry, which included independent research on the medicinal constituents of lavender and devil's club. He has studied at the School of Forest Medicine and under Sean Donahue. Croke can be found vending at the Olympia Farmer's Market, is the main medicine maker for the Olympia Free Herbal Clinic, leads classes around the PNW, and would love to help out in your garden.

GAIL FAITH EDWARDS is an internationally recognized Community Herbalist with more than thirty-five years of experience. Encouraging others to connect with nature in an intimate, healing, and reciprocal way is an essential theme of her work. She is the author of three books on herbal medicine, operates a vibrant medicinal herb farm, school, and herbal products business, and consults with clients. She has correspondence course students around the world. One of her great joys is leading the annual Earth & Spirit Tour to Southern Italy during which participants come into meaningful contact with our common, ancient spiritual history, culture, and inheritance. Some of the places Edwards has taught include the Sambhavana Clinic in Bhopal, India, the Garden of Minerva in Salerno, Italy, Yale School of Nursing, the University of Maine, and the College of the Atlantic. She is a mother of four grown children and a grandmother to three beautiful boys.

JESSE HATHAWAY DIAZ is a folklorist, diviner, artist, and performer living in New York City. With initiations in several forms of witchcraft from both Europe and the Americas, he is also a lifelong student of Mexican Curanderismo, an initiated olosha in the Lucumí orisha tradition, and a Tatá Quimbanda. He is half of www.wolf-and-goat.com, a store specializing in occult art, esoterica, and materia magica from many traditions including Traditional Craft and Quimbanda.

SHONAGH HOME is an author, shamanic practitioner, teacher, and public speaker. Her offerings focus on the cultivation of our intrinsic abilities—intuition, creativity, and multi-dimensional awareness. Her work with those in need is deeply probing and revelatory, breaking the spell and activating in the seeker an entirely new place of reference. In addition, Home is a beekeeper and apitherapist, administering bee venom therapy for a variety of illnesses such as MS and arthritis. She is an activist and a voice for the plight of the honeybees, offering a powerful solution in the form of biodynamic farming and gardening, as put forth by Rudolf Steiner. She is author of the books, *Ix Chel Wisdom: 7 Teachings from the Mayan Sacred Feminine; Love and Spirit Medicine;* and the forthcoming, *Honeybee Wisdom: A Modern Melissae Speaks.* Learn more at www.shonaghhome.com

MARCUS MCCOY is the originator of the bioregional animist practice and author of the original bioregional animism blog. He holds a BA in transpersonal anthropology in the study of the world's magical and spiritual systems. He is a student of plant teacher shamanry and a practitioner of many folk magic practices. McCoy is a magical herbalist, artist, distiller, and perfumer who founded and owns the House of Orpheus perfumery, a producer of talismanic and liminal perfumes, following and innovating the tradition of perfumerismo.

JULIE CHARETTE NUNN, CROW'S DAUGHTER is a shamanic herbalist, long-time teacher, herbal crafter, organic gardener/ farmer, goat herd, and successful business owner from Whidbey Island in Washington State. She teaches listening as a way to gain access to the abundant wisdom in nature, and supports people to open themselves to greater possibility by sharing their gifts. She offers shamanic herbal apprenticeships, classes, home study courses, and individual mentorship sessions in the shamanic herbal tradition of the wise woman. Nunn's specialty is connecting people in nature to learn more deeply who they are. www.crowsdaughter.com

CATAMARA ROSARIUM is a master herbalist, ritual artist, botanical alchemist, and proprietor of Rosarium Blends. Her extensive herbal experience is motivated by a deep attraction to plants, scents, and how they impact the senses. She has undertaken numerous unique training programs, including the Hermit's Grove Master Herbalism Program (Paul Beyerl), the Herbal Kingdom work at the Spagyricus Institute of Practical Alchemy (Robert Bartlett), Hoodoo and Rootwork (Catherine Yronwode), and the Arte of the Wortcunning Incense Tradition (Leon Reed). For the past seven years, Rosarium has co-organised the Esoteric Book Conference, and is the founder and convenor of the Viridis Genii Symposium. She has previously appeared in Sorita D'Este's Hekate anthology, *Her Sacred Fires* (2010). More information on her herbal work can be found on the Rosarium Blends website: www.rosariumblends.com

Running through the grass and climbing the acacia trees, RYAN WAZKA sprung forth from the Central Valley of California with a cactus in one hand and a reed-pipe in the other. Signaling all plants of the region to come enjoy the dance, a lesson has been shared and now a lesson grows. Several small booklets on the various grasses of the Pacific Northwest have been written and spread unto the winds of the world as a cosmic spore-print of information trickling into the stream of consciousness within the minds of the many. This is his first published piece, and one may discover other works of ethnobotanical research by this author in the future. He resides in the Pacific Northwest of the United States and travels aside the ocean, through the desert, and across the skies.

JENN ZAHRT holds a PHD in German literature and film from the University of California, Berkeley. Zahrt is a professional astrologer, writer, and an established editor of esoteric scholarship, including titles for Sophia Centre Press, Three Hands Press, and the journals *Culture and Cosmos*, CLAVIS, and *Diaphany*. Her trek on the green path began in November 2010, during a shamanic drumming ceremony in Marin County, California. In 2014 she spent three months living in the Cape Floral Region in South Africa, volunteering at a local organic farm and absorbing wisdom of the bioregion shared with her by amaPondo and Swazi sangomas, both in Cape Town and in their homesteads in the Transkei. She currently lives in Seattle. www.jennzahrt.com

ARTISTS:

MAXINE MILLER is a celebrated artist whose work centers around the Celtic and Pagan cultures. She has devoted many years of her artistic life to honoring and illuminating those traditions for people of today. Her work is rich with exquisite detail and symbolism. Celtic and Pagan practices are deeply connected to nature and the changing seasons. Ever since starting her first garden amidst the dingy decadence of her old Los Angeles neighborhood, Maxine began hearing the call of the plant spirits. She has remained fascinated and seduced by the beauty and variety of the plant world, and the cycles of life, death, and rebirth that define them. She now lives in the Pacific Northwest and is working on a book of her "Magical Botanical Series" illustrations.

LIV RAINEY-SMITH specializes in the superannuated art of hand-pulled xylographic prints. She prints her original wood-cut editions in Portland, Oregon, and shows at galleries and events regularly. Her publications include *Arcanum Bestiarum* from Three Hands Press, and *Starry Wisdom Library* from P.S. Publishing. She serves as Art Show Liaison for the Esoteric Book Conference in Seattle, Washington and volunteers with Print Arts Northwest. Rainey-Smith received her BFA from the Oregon College of Art and Craft in 2008.

Lightning Source UK Ltd.
Milton Keynes UK
UKOW01f1138240316

270797UK00001B/115/P

9 781943 710058